Light on the Path

SWAMI MUKTANANDA

Published by SYDA Foundation

Contents

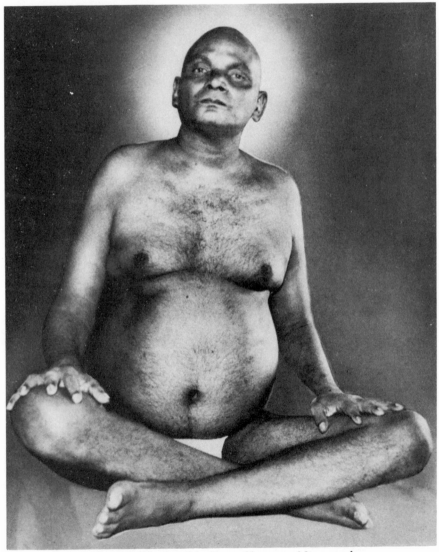

Swami Muktananda's Guru, Bhagavan Nityananda

Introduction

Self-realization is the supreme purpose and real meaning of life. When a person suffers from a sense of imperfection or lack of meaning in the material achievements of life, he longs for higher ideals and attainments. He keenly desires a fulfillment that is complete, constant, and indestructible. Such fulfillment is the highest realization.

Several articles by our beloved Gurudev, Swami Muk-tananda Paramahansa, explaining the way toward this highest realization are collectively published here for the benefit of seekers. Originally, they appeared in various is-sues of *Shree Gurudev-Vani*. They have also been published in Hindi under the title *Paramartha Prakash*.

The article "The Grace of the Guru" contains the es-sence of Baba's teachings. In it, he discusses the different paths to Self-realization, namely, *jnana, bhakti,* and *yoga*. Realization can be attained through any or a combination of these paths. However, the path of *gurukrupa,* or the grace of a true Guru, is the easiest of all. This path is also known as Siddha Yoga, of which this article is a very com-prehensive and lucid exposition. Baba often says, "I am not offering a novel theory or system. I would only like to make you experience in daily life what the great sages have preached and practiced since ancient times." What he means is that the knowledge and realization the saints achieved through severe ordeals can be attained in a spontaneous and natural manner by the grace of a Sadguru. He can reveal to us in an instant what would take a lifetime, perhaps many lifetimes, to attain through our own efforts.

A special feature of Baba's teachings is that he does not consider the world to be unreal or illusory. He describes it as a manifestation of Supreme Reality (Brahman), a projection of Chiti Shakti (divine Consciousness). Just as an artist paints various forms on the same canvas, with the same color and the same brush, similarly Chiti, in its immense joy of self-revelation, bursts forth in different forms and names as well as in different ways, including the thoughts arising in the human mind. Therefore, one need not be frightened or dismayed by the multitude of thought-waves that crowd the mind. One should regard these as a sport of the divine Consciousness because the mind is also one of its pulsations.

Another special feature of Baba's lectures and writings is that they are supported by the words of the scriptures and universally accepted saints, so that listeners and readers may be fully convinced that these are eternal truths.

The article "The Nature of God" is an example of Baba's catholic outlook. He says that God-realization is the same for all faiths. All differences are man-made, while God is above all divisions. He is the same for all, whether Hindus, Muslims, Christians, Sikhs, Parsis, or Jews. Only one God is the basis of the entire universe.

God has many names, and he can be addressed by any of them. He is with form and attribute, and without. He belongs to all faiths and sects, yet He is above them. The advocates of various religions have tried to describe Him according to their beliefs, but He remains the same— eternal, blissful, and the Truth. In this article, Baba has revealed his profound wisdom of Truth-realization and has described the nature of the Supreme Reality as *sat*, *chit*, and *ananda* in a way that seekers will easily understand.

In the article "Guru and Disciple," the nature of the grace-bestowing Guru is explained. A real Master is the embodiment of God's divine power. Having fully merged with God, he is His manifestation in physical form. Only such an enlightened soul is capable of bestowing grace on deserving aspirants. By the light of his ever-shining Spirit, the Guru touches and awakens the "sleeping" soul of his beloved disciple, and then the light of that highest Spirit also begins to shine in the disciple. One lamp is lighted from another lamp. This is known as *shaktipat*. A disciple can receive this great gift through single-minded devotion, total love, and constant service to his Guru. In short, the only key to attaining the Guru's grace is complete devotion to the Guru.

The theme of the article "The Nectar of Love for the Guru" is that a seeker who loves his Guru whole-heartedly and with complete devotion is able to see God embodied in his Guru. He who has tasted the nectar of the Guru's love feels his entire world to be fully merged with his Master. He does not have even the slightest attachment to any external thing or person. Baba says that the bliss, beauty, and enlightenment resulting from intense love for the Guru can be known only through experience. It cannot be adequately described. Thus, this article is a superb account of what a disciple can achieve by following the path of the Guru.

The article "Japa Yoga" explains how repetition of the mantra given by a Siddha Guru can also lead to the attainment of divine grace. This, too, is a form of Guru's grace. When the live mantra given by the Guru is repeated constantly, it descends from the tongue to the throat, from the throat to the heart, and from the heart to the navel. When this fourth stage is reached, repetition of the mantra becomes automatic. The unique process of Japa Yoga, which is borne out by actual experience, is described in detail in this article. Not only does it explain what is stated in the scriptures, but it also gives us first-hand knowledge of Baba's own rare experiences.

"The Path of Knowledge," which Baba wrote in Melbourne, Australia, adds the personal touch of his own example to the illuminating exposition of this path. In this article, Baba makes it clear that ultimately it is knowledge which dispels ignorance and brings salvation. Without knowledge, everything, including *japa, tapa,* silence, worship, and even meditation, is useless. But this knowledge does not manifest within oneself without *gurukrupa,* and for that, *guruseva,* or service to the Guru, is necessary.

Baba is one of the few living Gurus who is an adept in *shaktipat diksha.* Those who have received his grace know that he has, by his loving touch or glance, lighted the divine flame in many a pure-hearted and longing seeker. When a seeker receives *shaktipat,* he experiences an overflowing of bliss within and becomes ecstatic. Thus, by his divine power, Baba makes the seeker realize his true nature by giving him the experience of divinity within his own Self. In Baba's presence, all doubts and misgivings vanish, and one experiences inner contentment and a sense of fulfillment. The awakening of the divine energy through *shaktipat* manifests in various interesting ways. Some people hear melodious music within. Others see the Guru in the form of their chosen deity or some other god. Some see the Guru even if they are thousands of miles away and receive personal guidance from him. Some get a glimpse of their past lives.

There is such unique power in Baba's grace and such love in his personality that even his spoken or written words have great force and appeal. Many people have gone into deep meditation and experienced joyful peace while reading his words with complete absorption.

This collection of Baba's articles is being published with the hope that it will light the path for many who have sincerely embarked on the journey toward God.

— SWAMI PRAJNANANDA (AMMA)
Ganeshpuri, 1972

About
Swami Muktananda

Born in 1908 into a wealthy family in Mangalore, India, Swami Muktananda began his spiritual journey at the age of fifteen. A few years later he took the vows of a monk, and was given the title Swami and the name Muktananda.

For twenty-five years he traveled around India on foot, spending time with many of the renowned saints and meditation masters of his day. He mastered the classical systems of Indian philosophy, as well as Hatha Yoga and many other branches of spiritual and worldly science. In 1947 he met Bhagavan Nityananda, one of the great modern saints of India and a master of the Siddha tradition. After nine years of intense study under Nityananda's guidance, Muktananda reached the goal of spiritual practice, the state of Self-realization.

When Nityananda died in 1961, he passed on the power of the Siddha lineage to Muktananda. Since that time Swami Muktananda has made several trips to the West and has introduced Siddha meditation to hundreds of thousands of people. He has a large international following, and his students have established several hundred meditation centers around the world.

Swami Muktananda

1

The Grace
of the Guru

What is the ultimate goal of life and how can it be attained? Since ancient times the Hindu scriptures have expounded this theme. The seers of profound wisdom have said that to be entirely rid of pain, suffering, and sorrow and to attain the full measure of absolute bliss is the real goal of all beings.

Not only human beings but all creatures on this earth, from the tiniest to the largest, seek happiness and pleasure. Everyone strives in different ways for happiness, peace, plenty, and joy. It is for happiness that we manage factories and other enterprises, build houses, plant gardens, and raise families. For the same reason we pursue various arts, watch dramas, dress up, and enjoy feasts. In every aspect of daily life, our quest is for happiness. Thus, happiness is the real goal of a person's life.

Really speaking, in all these things we are seeking lasting happiness, but we do not know where and how to find it. The actual attainment of ceaseless, eternal bliss, which can be obtained by entering the realm of transcendental joy, is described as *moksha*, or God-realization. This is true religion. Religion is realization, and truly this is the highest purpose and ultimate goal of our life. It is true that we can experience supreme bliss in our own being, that we can realize the very essence of existence within and even transform our being into that highest essence. Therefore, it can be said that the attainment of supreme bliss is the highest goal of all human endeavor.

There are various means and systems in the world for attaining this goal. Different religious paths and philosophical systems have been enunciated by great seers. *Jnana*, yoga, *bhakti*, and the path of the Siddhas based on *guru-krupa*, the grace of the Guru, are chief among them. These paths are closely allied, yet each is singularly perfect and complete in itself. All religions, all paths, and all sects belong to the one Supreme Being and ultimately lead to Him alone.

JNANAMARGA
The Path of Knowledge

Knowledge is one of the means of attaining God-realization. It is knowing one's real Self by acquiring knowledge of the Truth in its essence through the teachings of a Guru. According to the *Bhagavad Gita*, the *Brahma Sutras*, and the Upanishads, the *chaitanya atman*, or conscious Self—which pervades everything without any distinction whatsoever, which is the sole support of everything, which having no support other than itself is ever perfect in itself and is self-existent, which, though residing in all the various types of bodies, does not assume those bodily forms, and which without changing its own true nature exists in everything as its own Self—is itself the indwelling soul of every being. That is the adorable Purushottama, the highest of all beings.

The *Vimarshini*, a commentary by Kshemaraja on the *Shiva Sutras*, defines *chaitanya atman* as

> chetayate iti chetanah
> sarvajñānakriyāsvatantrah
> tasya bhāvah chaitanyam.

That which imparts consciousness and possesses an
independent power of creation as well as knowledge
of all kinds—its state is known as *chaitanya*.

That ever-shining *chaitanya*, which is completely different
from the insentient, enters all things and brings them to
life, and although it assumes their various forms, it always
remains intangible. It is *alinga* (without any mark whatever)
and therefore unknowable. It is all-pervading, although it is
not visible to those without the eye of wisdom. It has
neither hands nor feet, yet it firmly holds all the elements
of the universe and travels everywhere. Sitting in perfect
steadiness, it proceeds afar to all quarters. To see without
eyes and to speak without tongue are its amazing glory and
greatness. With the winking of its eyes, the creation and
dissolution of the whole universe occur. Although it is ever
present in its fullness in the hearts of all human beings, it is
imperceptible to those who have not earned the grace of
the Guru; that is, it remains concealed. That highest
chaitanya is *satchidananda* (existence, consciousness, and
bliss), which in Vedanta is described as the ultimate goal of
life.

In short, the *chaitanya*, which imparts consciousness to
all yet remains aloof and absolutely independent, is itself
the various deities, and it alone is the Supreme Lord; truly,
it is the *atman*, or Self, seated in the hearts of all living
creatures. To know the *atman* through hearing (*shravana*)
and repeatedly reflecting on the teachings of the Guru
(*manana*), and then to become one with it through the
practice of meditation (*nididhyasana*), is the way of *jnanis*,
or followers of the path of knowledge.

While realizing the *atman*, a few truly fortunate ones in-
stantaneously become identical with that infinite, universal
chaitanya, in which they merge and melt their individ-
ualities, or their finite selves. This is like a droplet of water
becoming an ocean by losing its name, form, and identity
in the vastness of the ocean. But this comparison is in-

adequate, because the droplet of water loses name and
form, while the *atman* neither loses or abandons name and
form, nor regards them as unreal; by merging in Consciousness it merely transforms finite self into infinitude. That is,
a seeker, pursuing the path of knowledge as taught by the
Guru, merges his consciousness into the all-pervading Consciousness and thereby establishes his identity with that
chaitanya. Subsequently, he goes on repeating "I am That,
I am That" *(So'ham, So'ham)*, and also "I am the All;
all are mine." His "I" and the "All" become identical.
Thus, the *jnani* reaches a state in which he becomes free of
all distinctions such as internal and external, in which he is
without the sense of many and one, and in which his Self
experiences unity in diversity. Aloof from all, he attains
perfection. Seers, the wise ones, have described this state as
turiyatita or *nirvikalpa*, which is beyond anything that could
be expressed in words and which is no different from the
state of unity between *jiva*, the individual soul, and
Brahman, as visualized by the preceptors of the Advaita
philosophy in the well-known statement *(mahavakya)* from
the *Yajur Veda*, "I am Brahman" *(aham brahmasmi)*. This is
nothing but Vedanta. In the end, the absolutely unre-
stricted supreme bliss of oneness is obtained on this path.
After attaining divine bliss, the human soul rises above the
ordinary feelings of pleasure and pain and remains unaf-
fected by those transient states. After hearing all this, one
may feel that through the path of knowledge it is quite easy
to attain Self-knowledge, but in actual practice it is extremely difficult and attainable only by great effort and continuous endeavor. Nevertheless, one who is prepared to be
hanged or crucified tastes the divine nectar and attains immortality. The *Shvetashvatara Upanishad* (I, 11) says:

jñātvā devam sarvapāshāpahānihi.

Through knowledge of God, all fetters are destroyed.

YOGAMARGA
The Path of Concentration

Another means of attaining God-realization is yoga. Restraining the thought-waves that are continuously formed and modified in the mind is known as yoga. The word "yoga" comes from the Sanskrit root *yuj*, "to unite"; therefore, yoga also means uniting oneself with the Universal Consciousness. According to Maharshi Patanjali, one can achieve this by practicing eight phases of yoga, namely, *yama, niyama, asana, pranayama, pratyahara, dharana, dhyana,* and *samadhi.*

In this path of yoga, following *yama, niyama,* and other successive courses of discipline, one gathers together all one's scattered vital energies, both mental and physical, and brings them under one's control to achieve steadiness of the mind. As soon as the mind becomes calm and steady, an abundance of joy arises in the heart of the aspirant. This is the same as attaining the blissfulness described in Vedanta. Ultimately *jnana,* knowledge, becomes yoga, union. It can also be explained in this way: *Jnana,* which means knowing the Self as none other than the Supreme Reality, is the same as yoga, which means uniting the individual self with the Universal Consciousness, eternally pure, illumined, and ever free. This being so, Lord Krishna says in the *Bhagavad Gita* (V, 4–5):

> *sānkhyayogau pruthag bālāh pravadanti na panditāh;*
> *ekamapyāsthitah samyag ubhayor vindate phalam.*
> *yat sānkhyaih prāpyate sthānam tad yogairapi gamyate;*
> *ekam sānkhyam cha yogam cha yah pashyati sa pashyati.*

It is the ignorant and not the wise who speak of *jnana* and yoga as different. He who is rightly established even in one wins the fruit of both. The goal that the followers of *jnana* attain is also reached by the yogis. He sees truly who sees both *jnana* and yoga as one.

These words clearly explain that the final attainment is the same whether one follows the path of knowledge, which is a direct approach to Self-knowledge as propounded by Vedanta, or the path of yoga, which is a method of reaching the *nirvikalpa samadhi* through the practice of eightfold yoga.

Maharshi Patanjali formulated a very important work on the science of yoga called the *Yoga Sutras*. Patanjali is considered the highest authority on yoga, and the book, also known as *Yogadarshana*, is prescribed as a text for the systematic study of yoga. In a few aphorisms, Patanjali gives very useful directions for all spiritual aspirants. The *Yoga Sutras* do not contain theories which involve intellectual reasoning or controversial disputes; they are simply a practical treatise on the science of yoga.

This practical aspect of yoga first of all helps to make the body physically fit and strong by purifying its basic constituents. One may ask why so much importance is given to the body. I would say that a healthy body is absolutely essential for the practice of yoga. It is said that the body is the first and foremost means of practicing religion: *sharīramādyam khalu dharmasādhanam.* How can one be happy or feel comfortable if the body is sick or weak? How is the practice of religion or any form of spiritual discipline possible for such a one? Therefore, in the beginning, the very practical science of yoga not only emphasizes this point, but is even capable of making the human body strong and sturdy, provided that the instructions are strictly carried out. In the end, it elucidates in detail how, in the state of *samadhi,* one can attain an irrevocable union with the pure, undifferentiated Consciousness. The path of yoga is complete in itself. Even so, one is earnestly advised to have a teacher for proper guidance.

The third aphorism of the *Yoga Sutras* is *tadā drashtuh svarupe'vasthānam*—"At that time, the aspirant will be established in his own true nature." This is the highest ful-

fillment of yoga. When, after repeated attempts at concentration, a yogi succeeds in bringing all the modifications of
the mind under control, he sees his own true nature and
attains perfection, or supreme blessedness. To attain and to
be established in one's own real nature is the reward that
yoga grants to the yogi. In the *Bhagavad Gita* (VI, 46), the
Lord commands, *tasmād yogī bhavārjuna*—"Therefore, O
Arjuna, become a yogi." For this reason, it can be said that
even the Lord is in favor of the practice of yoga.

Besides Maharshi Patanjali, there were other seers, such
as Vyasa, Yajnavalkya, Kapilmuni, and Shvetashvatara,
who wrote on the unfathomable subject of yoga. The attainment of *yogananda,* the bliss one experiences when
united with God in a state of *samadhi* achieved through the
practice of concentration and meditation, is the main objective of yoga.

Many people are frightened by the idea of yoga. They
believe that yoga is meant for those who renounce their
households and live in a jungle or a cave, subsisting on
roots or tubers. This conception is entirely false. In fact,
yoga is an admirable way of life to be followed without fear
by everyone in the world.

All intelligent people, even if they are householders, can
practice yoga because it does not deny them a modest and
rational worldly life. In fact, yoga is complementary to such
a life and, in time, becomes a friend to it.

Actually, the eight constituents of yoga are already being
practiced, at least in part, in daily life. For example, *yama*
and *niyama* in a broad sense mean the observance of certain
rules of conduct. *Asana* means sitting in a particular posture. *Dhyana* means concentration. Are not rules and regulations observed in worldly life? Does one not sit in a proper
manner? Can an artist, a sculptor, a watchmaker, or an
engineer perform his work properly without concentrating
and without forming an image of the final product before
his mental eye? Can anyone be crowned with success with-

out planning anything in the mind at the outset? Without steadying his mind, can a student concentrate on his studies or pass his examinations? Can anyone have a sound sleep without making the mind free of thoughts and anxieties? Of course not. Yoga teaches us the same things: how to concentrate, how to make the mind steady and free of thoughts, and how to train and cultivate the mind in order to become absorbed in a goal. The instances given above very clearly show how the different parts of yoga are used or practiced in daily life. Nor is this practice limited to the physical and mental planes alone. It extends as well to the moral aspect. *Satya*, one of the moral disciplines, means truthfulness. Is not a wife truthful and loyal in her dealings with her husband? Is she not always honest with him?

Nowadays, many hospitals are filled with the sick. Why? The primary reason is that most people today lead a disorderly and irregular life. Those who lead a life in conformity with the rules laid down in the science of health are immune from suffering and paying visits to physicians. A sound body and good health are of utmost value. They are real wealth. Regular habits and a balanced way of life are yoga put into practice. Yoga teaches these regulations and a way of life that is very conducive to good health. Thus, yoga chases away all one's weaknesses. It creates heaven on earth by transforming all ugliness into celestial beauty. Yoga is therefore a peerless friend of both the worldly-minded and the spiritually inclined. It should be practiced daily, regularly, and with respect.

BHAKTIMARGA
The Path of Devotion

Intense love of God is known as *bhakti*, or devotion. Like *jnana* and yoga, *bhakti* is a means to God, perfect in itself.

The way of love is the sweetest, like nectar. *Premananda, purnananda, yogananda, satchidananda, brahmananda*—all these terms convey the same meaning, namely, the enjoyment of perfect bliss. On attaining Self-knowledge, the *jnani* comes to realize that the entire world, full of movable and immovable entities, is nothing but the manifestation of the one Supreme Reality. Knowing this, he becomes free from all duality, such as pain and pleasure, love and hate, likes and dislikes. Then within his innermost Self he becomes the subject of perfect bliss and is ecstatic. When a yogi, through the practice of *yama, niyama, pranayama,* and *dhyana,* succeeds in attaining the state of mindlessness, he experiences the same supreme bliss which the *jnani* experiences through Self-knowledge. Thus, the yogi is intoxicated by *yogananda,* the *jnani* is absorbed in *jnanananda,* and similarly the *bhakta* becomes enraptured in *premananda.* This is the ecstatic delight of love of all the love-stricken devotees of God.

The goal may seem to differ because the approaches are different in the paths of *jnana,* yoga, and *bhakti;* but this is not so, for even *bhaktas* love and adore the eternal, imperishable, perfect Brahman alone. In the *Shrimad Bhagavat Purana* (X, 14, 32) it is said:

> *aho bhāgyamaho bhāgyam nandagopavrajaukasām;*
> *yanmitram paramānandam pūrnabhrahma sanātanam.*

> Oh, how great is the fortune of Nanda and the other cowherds living in Vraja since Lord Krishna, the imperishable, perfect Brahman, full of bliss, is their friend.

Is there a place or a person without love? How can there be love where there is no *rasa* (essence of joy)? The very core and nature of God is love, bliss, and ecstasy. The *Taittiriya Upanishad* (II, 7) says, *raso vai sah; rasam hyevāyam labdhvā'nandī bhavati*—"Truly God is *rasa* and truly, on obtaining the *rasa,* one becomes blissful." The *Taittiriya Upanishad* further says (III, 6):

ānandād hi eva khalvimāni bhūtāni jāyante,
ānandena jātāni jīvanti,
ānandam prayantyabhisamvishanti.

All these beings are indeed born from bliss; being
born they live by bliss, and after death they enter
into bliss.

It is from bliss that the world is created, maintained, and
destroyed. That God Himself is the cause of creation was
unequivocally accepted by the philosophers who founded
the six systems of Indian philosophy. The cause (God) is
inseparably entwined with its effect (creation). From all
this, it is clear that love is the original cause or source of
creation, for one grows by love, lives by love, and finally
even merges into eternal love. Love is all-pervading. To
aspire to the Divine would, therefore, mean to love the
Divine.

Knowing his beloved God to be present everywhere and
seeing Him in all things, a *bhakta* leads his life happily and
contentedly. Such a devotee creates a veritable heaven
wherever he happens to be. Whatever is seen by the eyes,
the lover perceives as his charming Beloved; whatever is
heard by the ears, the lover recognizes as the gentle voice of
the Beloved. With his tongue he continuously chants the
sweetest melodies of love in praise of the Beloved, and his
entire body feels the softest touch of his Beloved. A drop of
water in the midst of an ocean beholds nothing but water
on all sides. Similarly, a *bhakta* perceives God everywhere
and rejoices. How does one gain such sight and such joy?
The means to behold Him in this way are the incessant
singing of devotional songs and rendering of loving service,
which are made possible by merging the entire heart and
mind, together with the intellect, ego, and senses, with the
Beloved. Immortal joy is the final achievement.

This immortal joy can, however, be obtained only by the
grace of great souls. In the *Narada Bhakti Sutras* (39) it is
said:

mahatsangastu durlabho'gamyo'moghashcha.

The company of the great is incomprehensible, in-fallible, and difficult to attain.

It is not easy to come in contact with such beings, and it is even more difficult to be a recipient of their grace. Nevertheless, without the grace of a man of God, a devotee cannot become a true lover of God. Through direct contact with godlike saints and their loving influence, the path of love can become easy.

So far, we have seen three different ways of attaining the ultimate goal of Self-realization: *jnana*, yoga, and *bhakti*. A person can reach his spiritual goal by the practice of one or all three of these means. Although these paths differ from each other, the spiritual aspirants of each one can arrive at the same goal and attain the same immortal state. But these means are very difficult and wearisome, because one has to suffer a great deal of hardship before attaining liberation and supreme bliss. The *Katha Upanishad* says:

kshurasya dhārā nishitā duratyayā
durgam pathastatkavayo vadanti.

Sages declare that the path is difficult and hard to traverse, like the sharpened edge of a razor.

The road to supreme knowledge is extremely narrow, and so it is compared to a razor's edge. The path is so arduous that one Hindi poet says it is like chewing peanuts made of steel. The Lord Himself says in the *Bhagavad Gita* (VII, 19) that even a *jnani* attains the state of supreme bliss only after the hard work of many lives:

bahūnām janmanāmante jnānavān mām prapadyate.

A *jnani* attains Me at the end of many births.

This being the case, a seeker may wonder whether there is any other way to the final goal besides these three. There is indeed a way. It is an easy discipline which one acquires from a Sadguru. If he is gracious and his kind favor descends upon a seeker, the entire path of *sadhana* becomes simple, comprehensive, and effortless. It is known as the path of the Siddhas.

SIDDHAMARGA
The Path of the Perfect Ones

This easiest and surest means to the goal is also known as *gurukrupa*, the grace of a perfect Master. By the grace of a Sadguru, a true and earnest disciple turns an inaccessible path of *sadhana* into an easy way to proceed on the spiritual journey. Once he has been initiated by the Sadguru, his path is automatically rendered smooth, clear, and easy to practice.

Shaktipat Diksha

In every sect or religion there is a tradition of *diksha*, or initiation. The real meaning of *diksha* is "to give"—to give an awakening whereby the initiated one can have a super-conscious vision of the Lord and ultimately experience his identity with that Supreme Self.

The grace of the Guru is itself a process of initiation known as *shaktipat diksha*. This is the same process of grace whereby Shri Ramakrishna Paramahansa gave a direct experience of divinity to Swami Vivekananda the moment he touched him. Indeed, the process of *shaktipat diksha* is highly mysterious, secret, and amazing. It is a very ancient tradition practiced in India. The following are three typical illustrations of *shaktipat diksha:* (1) the bestowing of grace by means of which Shri Gahininath, in an instant, made Shri Nivrittinath realize the highest Brahman; (2) the transmission of divine Shakti which happened when Kabir Sahib was accidentally touched by Shri Ramanandaji and which brought about within Kabir a spontaneous awakening of intense love and devotion for God; (3) the secret process by which Shankaracharya, just by casting a glance at Hastamalaka, made him a knower of the Self. The first illustration is one of *manasa diksha* (by the will of the Sadguru), the second is of *sparsha diksha* (by the touch of the Sadguru), and the third is of *druk diksha* (by the glance of the Sadguru).

Swami Shankar Purushottam Tirth, the Shankaracharya of Govardhan Math, knew its secret and was thoroughly proficient in initiating by *shaktipat diksha*. His book *Yogavani* (written in Bengali and in Hindi) is an authentic treatise on the subject. In the *Gheranda Samhita, Vayaviya Samhita, Skanda Purana, Kularnava Tantra, Yogini Tantra, Agama Sandarbha, Sharada Tilaka,* as well as in the books of the Shaiva, Vaishnava, and Saura paths and in certain yogic Upanishads, the subject is dealt with fully. Even among the *lamas* of Tibet this is a customary practice, but not everyone is familiar with it. People with partial and superficial conceptions do not know the subject well enough, and they err.

Mahaprabhu Shri Gauranga, out of his divine mercy and love, even initiated several bad characters like Nauroji, a notorious thief, and Lakshmibai and Satyabai, two courtesans. After Shri Gauranga Prabhu aroused divine love in their hearts, they turned toward God and spent the rest of their lives in devotion.

There are those who doubt the efficacy of *shaktipat*. Some deluded people misinterpret it as a tantric *sadhana*. This is sheer ignorance. Others think that it is either a practice of *vama marga*, the left-handed path, or a mode of worship of Shakti which is not considered valid by the scriptures. Being misinformed, though erudite scholars, they are on a false path and do not know the slightest secret of *shaktipat*. On hearing the word *shakti*, they presume it has something to do with *shaktas* (worshippers of Shakti) and thus remain far away from true God-realization. For countless ages, *shaktipat* has been used as a secret means of initiation by the great sages. To transmit one's own glory and luster of divine enlightenment into a disciple and give him an instantaneous, direct experience of Brahman, the Eternal Spirit, is the secret meaning of *shaktipat.*

To explain this, I will narrate a true story. In Marathawada, there is a town named Ambajogai, a place of pilgrimage famous for its temple Jogai-ki-Amba. Once Jaitrapal, the ruling king of the region, went on horseback to a yogi named Mukundrai and insisted that the yogi show him the Supreme in the short time required to mount a horse with one leg already in the stirrup. At this obstinacy, by one slash of the king's own whip, Mukundrai made the king realize the Supreme Reality. By the power acquired through austerities, sages can either bless or curse. In the same way, it is neither impossible nor difficult for them to transmit spiritual energy to a disciple on the strength of their divine knowledge. It is bound to be experienced by earnest and sincere aspirants on the spiritual path.

In every human being there dwells a divine energy, the Kundalini Shakti. This energy has two aspects: One manifests *samsara,* the ephemeral worldly existence; the other leads to the highest Truth. When the Guru transmits his soul power to a disciple, the latter aspect of the Kundalini Shakti is automatically activated in the disciple and set into operation. This is known as *shaktipat diksha* or *gurukrupa.*

That energy, which has the supreme capacity to create the universe independently, is called Chiti Shakti. This pure Consciousness, which is full of absolute bliss, dwells in the Guru in its fullness. Assuming the three different aspects of unity, diversity, and unity in diversity, creating the universe of manifold forms out of one, and manifesting many in one and one in many, Chiti Shakti reveals an ever-changing world in the *atman,* which is a changeless

reality. This active energy has many names—Chiti, Maha-
maya, Shiva's Gauri, Narayana's Lakshmi, Rama's Sita,
Krishna's Radha, the yogi's Kundalini, the poet's inspiration, and the blissful stream of joy of the *atman*—and
an infinite number of aspects. This divine energy is not in
any way different from or independent of the highest Reality. Both the Reality and its divine energy are one and the
same, just as a king and his ruling power go together.

When the attributeless, formless, changeless Reality
which underlies the entire universe, and which is the pure,
ultimate Consciousness, is stirred up, this divine energy begins to operate in it. She is the power of becoming, released
out of the Eternal Being and expressing Herself through all
names, all forms, and all changes that we call the world.
Indeed, She is the most magnificent power — Shri Kundalini Shakti — of the Supreme Reality. To set this Kundalini
into operation within an individual being is known as *shaktipat,* and one who gives *shaktipat diksha* is a Guru. The *Yoga
Vasishtha* says:

> darshanāt sparshanāt shabdāt
> krupayā shishyadehake;
> janayedyah samāvesham
> shāmbhavam sa hi deshikaha.

> He who, by his gracious look, touch, or word, gives
> to the disciple an experience of his identity with
> the Absolute is indeed the Guru.

In the *Kularnava Tantra* it is said:

> guroryasyaiva samsparshāt
> parānando'bhijāyate;
> gurum tameva vrunuyāt
> nāparam matimānnaraha.

> A discriminating person should choose as his Guru
> none else but one by whose touch he experiences
> the highest bliss.

Experiences of the Awakened Kundalini

After a disciple is initiated by such a Guru, various types of internal activities occur. Some disciples experience great joy, while others become either apparently dull and stupefied, or restless. With certain disciples a variety of strange bodily reactions, such as yogic postures, gestures, tremors, or dancing poses, begin to take place involuntarily in every part of the body. This may cause wonder. Some disciples get frightened. For a short period of time, one may feel pain in almost every part of the body. Various stirrings may occur in the heart, head, and abdomen; and throbbing of the muscles and fascinating, thrilling sensations may be experienced. One may feel drowsy and may even enter a state of deep meditation without making any effort. When a disciple begins to see lights of different colors—red, white, black, and azure—in meditation, his joy increases day by day, and he follows his spiritual discipline with greater enthusiasm. Sometimes during meditation one may see temples, mountains, caves, and even other worlds. Thereafter, a divine light of indescribable luster is always visible during meditation. That light is considered to be the light of the qualified, or manifested, Reality (*saguna* Brahman). The *Pashupata-brahma Upanishad* describes it in this way:

> *akalpitodbhavam jyotih svayam jyotih prakāshitam;*
> *akasmād drushyate jyotis tajjyotih paramātmani.*

> The light does not appear by any pre-imagination, but is manifested by itself. Such self-resplendent light is seen unexpectedly during meditation. The light which thus makes itself evident exists in the Supreme Self.

Other worlds are also seen in this divine light, and the disciple comes to know that Pitruloka (the world of the ancestors), Chandraloka (the world of the moon), and Devaloka (the world of the gods) actually exist.

Various emotions (*ashtabhava*) may be automatically awakened. Overwhelmed, the disciple swims in an ocean of infinite bliss, filled with joy and delight. Day by day, as his zeal and fervor increase, the disciple has countless experiences. With each new vision and divine experience, his steadfastness and enthusiasm in the practice of discipline grow, which helps him to continue with added vigor. If he follows the proper rules of conduct, such a seeker may carry out his daily routine or worldly dealings, may visit and stay in any part of the country, and yet, due to his intense faith, see and feel the presence of his adorable Guru everywhere. Be assured that this is no myth, nor am I writing about magic. Rather, it is an unmistakable fact that the Supreme Spirit is truly and eternally all-pervasive and has penetrated every atom of the visible universe. This Self, as Consciousness, permeates the entire world of the animate and inanimate, sentient and insentient. This is explained in the *Shiva Sutra Vimarshini*:

> *tadeva bhavati sthūlam sthūlopādhivashātpriye;*
> *sthūlasūkshmavibhedena tadekam samvyavasthitam.*

> O beloved, That itself becomes the gross by conditioning itself into the gross. That alone exists in the different gross and subtle entities.

Just as the Universal Consciousness (Chiti), by limiting itself, becomes the individual consciousness (*chitta*), similarly the sentient (*chetan*) changes itself to appear insentient (*jada*). That is, the highly luminous Self, while manifesting itself as gross entities, becomes conditioned and limited in the form of diverse objects. The pervasive Self becomes the pervaded. Therefore, the pervaded is not separate from the pervasive because the pervader and the things pervaded by Him are the same, not different. I am reminded of a saint's poem:

> Whether I call you an earring or an anklet,
> a brooch or bracelet,

the inherent gold glitters brightly in you.
So is the Self seen shining through everything.

There are other analogies that explain this. The physical body, heterogeneous as it is, is formed from one drop of semen. Throughout cotton fabric, there is nothing but cotton threads; in the fabric there are threads, and in the threads there is cotton. Similarly, the Lord, the Supreme Spirit, is the basis of everything, including the movable and the immovable entities of this universe. Therefore, the universe itself is the cosmic Self.

I will give one more illustration. A steamer leaving the Bombay dock is on the sea until it reaches the port of Mangalore. The steamer is not at any moment separated from the sea. In the same way, aspirants who have been initiated by *shaktipat* dwell in that one Universal Consciousness— Chiti—whether they carry on their spiritual practices at one end of the world or the other. It is therefore not at all surprising if they see their Guru or their chosen deity in visions even when they are thousands of miles away, because just as the steamer is always in the water until it reaches the port, so also the indwelling *chaitanya* is always with aspirants in all places, at all times, and under all conditions. *Chaitanya* is uniform everywhere because it is all-pervading. All this is absolutely true.

In the *Tantrasara*, it is said that the Lord's Shakti is full of infinite wonders: *tachchamatkāra ichchhāshaktihi*. It is She who wills various yogic processes in *sadhakas* (seekers). Then an array of wonderful yogic *asanas*, *mudras*, and different types of meditation take place. These yogic exercises cleanse the nervous system. Generally, by the process of *nadishuddhi* (purification of the subtle channels within the body) many diseases and ailments are cured. Many types of *pranayama* are also performed automatically. These open up all the *chakras* (psychic nerve centers), and thus, in a very simple and easy manner, the passage in the *sushumna* is cleared of all obstructions. The *prana* rising through the *sushumna* is stabilized upon reaching the *sahasrara,* the spiritual center at the crown of the head. This process of *nadishuddhi* goes on until the *prana* and *apana* are finally equalized. It is said in the Shiva Sutras (III, 22) that with the equalizing of *prana* the spiritual aspirant sees equality everywhere: *pranasamachare samadarshanam.* Then he becomes a perfect yogi, for his intellect abandons all sense of the limited "I" and realizes its oneness with the all-pervading cosmic intelligence. In this connection, the *Spanda Karika* (II, 30) says:

iti va yasya samvittih kridatvenakhilam jagat;
sa pashyansatatam yukto jivanmukto na samshayah.

He who knows and regards the entire world as a sport of the Divine, being ever united with the Universal Consciousness, is without doubt liberated even while alive.

A spiritual aspirant blessed by the Guru's grace becomes filled with joy upon recognizing this active world as nothing but the projection of the divine, cosmic Kundalini. If he follows the right path, such an aspirant can lead a normal worldly life; it is not necessary for him to leave his household. Through visions, his awakened Kundalini always protects him. She fulfills all his wishes and aspirations. Nothing remains to be obtained by him in whose heart this Shakti enters.

This Shakti is described by Parashiva Himself in the *Shiva Sutras* (I, 13): *ichchhashaktiruma kumari* — "*Icchashakti,* the power of will, is the ever-young maiden called Uma." The *Shiva Sutra Vimarshini* explains:

sa cha kumari vishvasargasamharakridapara.

That young lady is ever engrossed in the sport of creation and destruction of the universe.

The Shakti, the active aspect of the Supreme Lord, which brings about the creation, continued existence, and absorption of the universe, is the Supreme Shakti Uma, also described in the *Shiva Sutra Vimarshini* as follows: *paraiva pārameshvarī svātantryarūpā*—"She is absolute and of independent will." She creates an infinite number of worlds out of nothing. She is the same Shakti which is awakened in a disciple by the Guru's grace. Can any spiritual practices be difficult for those whose Kundalini is awakened by the Guru's grace? Even salvation is within their easy reach. Such favored ones practice the easiest of the easy means of discipline. The power of *gurukrupa* always saves them from degradation. Indeed, Kundalini automatically fills their hearts with supreme bliss, as described in the *Tantrasara: svātantryamānanda shaktihi*. When this bliss-showering Kundalini, which rises forth spontaneously without ever needing the help of any object or means, awakens in a spiritual aspirant, not only is he delighted, but he becomes the very embodiment of supreme bliss.

The Shakti alone knows Herself, and She alone is fully aware of Her own true nature, as distinctly expressed in the *Tantrasara: āmarshātmakatā jnānashaktihi*. She is the power which, while holding and containing the entire cosmos, ever rests in blissful merriment and is full of consciousness and intelligence. Nothing is unattainable to those in whom this Shakti becomes active because, as described in the *Tantrasara*, She is able to assume any form She likes: *sarvākārayogitvam kriyāshaktihi*. The *Shiva Sutras* (III, 30) say that this Shakti is capable of creating many worlds on Her own screen, without any outside material: *svashaktiprachayo'sya vishvam.*

As we have seen, Chiti, which is the same as Parameshvari Yogamaya Kundalini, ever flashes forth, manifesting the universe of infinite forms with absolute independence by Her own power. When, by the Guru's grace, this divine Shakti becomes active in the heart of spiritual aspirants, salvation loses all its meaning, because they themselves become one with Chiti. This should not be at all surprising since the entire universe is, in fact, Chiti. The *sadhaka, sadhana,* Guru, mantra, *prana,* and *kriya* are all abounding in Chiti. Chiti is the five elements, namely, ether, air, fire, water, and earth. All animals are full of Chiti. Truly, in every aspect, Chiti alone is the cause and effect of the universe:

> *chitih vishvam sādhayati,*
> *chitimāsādya vishvam bhavati,*
> *chityām vishvamīshvarah karoti,*
> *chiteh vishvam bhavati,*
> *chiteh vikāro vishvam bhavati,*
> *chitau vishvam sthitamiti.*

Chiti creates the universe; the universe comes into existence with the help of Chiti; God creates the universe in Chiti; the universe is created from Chiti; the universe is the modification of Chiti; the universe is stationed in Chiti.

Therefore, in this world, which is permeated by Chiti, there is no real impediment to becoming that Chiti by the grace of the Guru.

Final Attainment

All the Vedas say that "this Self is Brahman" *(ayamātmā brahma).* If, therefore, the entire universe is nothing but the Lord Himself, it is the absolute truth that one can experience divine bliss, or Universal Consciousness, by following the path shown by the Guru. This is precisely the gift and teaching of Bhagavan Shri Nityananda. The *Shiva Sutra Vimarshini* states:

> *gururvā pārameshvarī anugrāhikā shaktihi.*

The Guru is the grace-bestowing power of the Supreme Lord.

At the time of initiation, it is the Guru who, in the form of Shakti, enters the disciple. Soon after this, the disciple's entire personality is transformed. From the *muladhara chakra* at the base of the spinal column to the *sahasrara* in the crown of the head, the Shakti performs innumerable strange activities; but She resides in the heart of the disciple, so that he is always aware of Her work and activities.

While in meditation, aspirants sometimes perceive funeral pyres burning and everything around them in flames. Some aspirants, out of fear, think of getting up from meditation and running away, but when they open their eyes, they see no fire. These and other similar experiences are real spiritual experiences and not mere illusions. Thereafter, the blazing fire changes into a saffron or golden light of divine beauty and remains visible almost until the attainment of perfection. In this light *sadhakas* often have visions of saints and sages, and some even receive divine mantras or herbs from Siddhas. Such mantras can bring about spiritual awakening in anyone, and such medicinal herbs can cure incurable diseases. Not all aspirants are favored with such divine gifts, but one who is so blessed no doubt becomes a great benefactor of humanity.

The aspirant next begins to hear different kinds of divine music. As he continues to listen to it intently, he develops the power of effortless concentration and becomes absorbed in the music itself. When he merges into the divine sound (*nada*) and reaches a state of thoughtlessness, he experiences great joy, bliss, and peace. Through the constant linking of the mind to the divine sound, the aspirant reaches a stage at which he becomes free from all feelings of separateness, such as mine and yours, one and many. Then, having transcended the three ordinary states of waking, dream, and deep sleep, he remains in the fourth state of *turiya*, the transcendental state, where he becomes fully youthful and enjoys extraordinary bliss and profound tranquility called *turiyananda*. The *Shiva Sutras* (I, 7) say:

jāgratsvapnasushuptabhede turyābhogasambhavaha.
Apparently being in one of the three states of waking, dreaming, or deep sleep, he ever abides in the
turiya state.

This is the fruit of yoga attainable by *gurukrupa.*
This yoga is also known as Siddha Yoga because it is
accomplished only through a Siddha (a perfect yogi).
Without the grace of a Siddha, it is very difficult to reach
the superconscious state, even through the practice of yoga.
This path is also known as Maha Yoga, the great yoga,
because the essence of all yogas is included in it. Therefore,
this approach to the Ultimate is called Siddha Yoga, Maha
Yoga, Purna Yoga, Parashiva Yoga, or *gurukrupa.*

By the Guru's grace, the unrivaled One, who is all-
blissful, is revealed. This direct comprehension and immediate experience are amazing to the yogi and are spoken
of in the *Shiva Sutras* (I, 12): *vismayo yogabhūmikāhā*—"The
successive stages of yoga are full of wonders."

At the completion of this yoga, at its ultimate fulfillment, the yogi becomes equal to Shiva, as stated in the
Shiva Sutras (III, 25): *shivatulyo jāyate*—"He becomes like
Shiva." Just as a worm is transformed into a wasp by the
contact of a wasp, or as water when poured into milk becomes milk, so also, by the touch or grace of the Guru and
by the union of Shiva and Shakti in the *sahasrara, jiva*—the
soul with limited consciousness—becomes Shiva—the omniscient, omnipotent Absolute Being. That perfected yogi
forgets about his family, caste, creed, race, and even the
consciousness of his own body. Instead, the awareness of
being one with Shiva (*Shivo'ham*) starts repeating itself in
his heart.

After being initiated by the Guru, an earnest disciple, on
continuing his spiritual practices regularly for a period of
three, six, nine, or twelve years (the period depending on
the disciple's caliber, purity of heart, intensity of practice,
and spiritual development), is able to experience divinity

within his own Self. Thus, he becomes Self-realized. The Mahashakti Kundalini, always residing in the heart of a yogi, gives him many wonderful experiences and molds him according to Her will. On one yogi She bestows poetic genius, and to another She gives erudition and wisdom. She may bathe a third in the ecstatic stream of divine love. All people in close association with such blessed yogis enjoy peace and happiness. Even nature is enamored of them for, wherever they stay, the trees and creepers grow luxuriantly, orchards bear fruit in plenty, flower gardens blossom in marvellous beauty, and fields yield the best of harvests. The surrounding groves and woodlands always remain green and are as refreshing and charming as celestial gardens. Wherever Parashiva's Shakti, which manifests and expands the universe, is active, the trees and the foliage, fruits, and flowers bloom in abundance very naturally. It is true that the entire atmosphere around such yogis vibrates with joy, abounds with love, and is pervaded by their Shakti. Whoever goes there with love, devotion, and faith experiences the divine influence and radiation of the Shakti and feels peaceful within. All these wonders are due to the munificence of Maha Yoga.

After entering the *sushumna*, the Mahashakti Kundalini reveals Her supernatural qualities, such as joy, strength, peace, and bliss, to the aspirant. Then he carries out his spiritual exercises with enthusiasm. Inspired by the evernew and mysterious experiences of the Kundalini, he practices yoga regularly and punctually. Soon he feels the spontaneous rising of divine love within his heart. Just as an addict cannot give up his habit and is restless until he secures his daily dose of intoxicant, a student of Siddha Yoga cannot be calm and restful without his daily practice of spiritual discipline. As the seeker follows this regular practice, the Kundalini, which is seated in the *muladhara*, gradually travels upward, piercing the *chakras* on Her way, until She reaches the *sahasrara*, the thousand-petaled lotus

in the crown of the head. Here, in the last phase of Her
active form, she unites with Her Lord Shiva and becomes
one with Him. When the Kundalini Shakti is thus pacified
by uniting with Shiva in the *sahasrara*, She becomes static.
One who has completed the full course of yoga *sadhana* is a
perfect yogi. When, in this way, the Kundalini Shakti is
thoroughly stilled in the *sahasrara*, pure knowledge arises.
The *Shiva Sutras* (I, 21) state that with the dawning of pure
knowledge one attains the perfection of the Supreme Lord:
shuddhavidyodayāchchakreshatva-siddhihi. Thereafter, the
yogi forgets his spiritual striving and remains ever absorbed
in the supreme state. When he was under the veil of ignorance, he felt miserable, poor, imperfect, attached, and
powerless; but after the awakening of the divine Shakti, he
realizes that he is perfect, accomplished, nonattached,
powerful, filled with love, and of divine nature. In the joy
of his attainment, he utters, "I am bliss" (*ānando'ham*).
Drinking a fresh cup of joy every day, he remains in a state
of deep intoxication. Now he no longer suffers from the
dual malady of birth and death, for they dare not appear
before him.

Those whose divine Kundalini Shakti is awakened naturally become fully drunk by sipping from the spontaneous
fountain of bliss within. Just as a drop of water that has
fallen into the ocean sees water on all sides and, merging
with it, acquires vast expanse and loses its separate existence, so also the yogi, in the spontaneity of his inner joy,
visualizes himself as the Universal Spirit pervading the entire world and ultimately attains profound peace and repose
in it. How one feels upon reaching this state is expressed in
the following verse from the *Ishvarapratyabhijna* (I, 12):

> *sarvo mamāyam vibhava ityevam parijānatah;*
> *vishvātmano vikalpānām prasare'pi maheshatā.*

> He who has realized that the entire universe is his
> Self, and knows that "all this glory of manifestation
> is mine," possesses the power of the Supreme Lord

even though different thoughts may play in his mind.

A yogi who perceives the great visible universe as a grand sport of his own Self or of the Supreme Spirit remains in the unchanging state of true knowledge, even though he may perceive differences. He sees the unfolding of Parashiva being manifested in all entities. He perceives Shiva in front and behind, above and below, and on all sides. He knows nothing except Shiva. He himself becomes Shiva. To him:

shivo dātā shivo bhoktā shivam sarvam idam jagat;
shivo yajati yajnashcha yah shivam so'ham eva hi.

Shiva is the giver and Shiva is the enjoyer. Shiva is this entire universe. Shiva is the sacrificer and the sacrifice. "I am that Shiva."

2

The Nature of God

God, the Supreme Being, the One without a second, is known by more than one name, and there are many paths and forms of *sadhana* to reach Him. God is infinite and so are His names. Yogis call Him *Om; jnanis* call Him *So'ham* ("I am That"); some say He is *prajna* (pure wisdom); some say He is *chaitanya* (Consciousness); and so on. One does not need a term to name the Nameless, but all these different names refer to the same entity called God. He is the Supreme Reality which the Upanishads call Brahman. Brahman can never be defined or described. It has no attributes but is of the nature of *sat, chit,* and *ananda* (existence, consciousness, and bliss).

Different creeds and sects put forth various arguments and use every imaginable kind of logic to establish their own concept of God. Let anyone say anything; nevertheless, it is absolutely true that God does exist and that He is *satchidananda.*

All dogmatic preachers of religion have conceived of, described, and presented that *satchidananda* in a form which suits their own belief or conception. Some seek Him in the form of Lord Vishnu, love incarnate; others call Him Sadashiva, the embodiment of peace; some think of Him as a void, beyond the reach of the mind; and others describe Him as the supremely blissful Brahman. In fact, everyone's concept of God conforms to his own attainment, and therefore these views should be regarded as correct, but partial. However, *satchidananda* stands out as the truest and the closest description of the Godhead, which is an incomprehensible and indescribable Beyond.

There are also various arguments for and against the form and the formless nature of God. But the nature of the incomprehensible Supreme Lord does not need proof by arguments. Being all-powerful, it is certainly not difficult for the Formless to assume form for some specific purpose. If this attributeless, formless God can create the world with its numerous hills and dales, rivers and seas by His own greatness, it should not be at all difficult for Him to assume the physical forms that have come to be known as Rama, Krishna, Buddha, Christ, Mohammed, and so on. Thus, it is easy for the Unmanifest to become manifest in any form.

It is unnecessary to argue whether God has any attributes. Each devotee can, and should, worship Him according to his own approach, feeling, and sentiment. The amount of divine happiness derived by a devotee depends entirely on the intensity of his own feelings. Pure sentiment always brings high rewards. Some years ago in Maharashtra, there lived a saintly woman called Bahinabai. She was a Self-realized soul who worshipped Truth and saw everything in its proper perspective. In one of her poems she wrote, "Intense devotion begets the desired fruits and ultimately leads to salvation." The words of the Vedas, that even fire can be kindled by intensity of will, devotion, and faith, are true. Bhagavan Nityananda used to say that a devotee can perceive God in his own heart by pure devotion and faith.

God is kind, compassionate, and also generous in bestowing His grace. In order to realize that merciful One, a seeker must follow any one of the spiritual paths and follow the disciplines prescribed therein with an earnest heart. But at the same time, we must remember that it is not fair to consider all other paths and disciplines inferior to our own.

Bigotry cannot please God, because He is never captivated by any ritual or any particular method of *sadhana*. It is only out of compassion that He reveals Himself to devotees when He is pleased by their selfless love. One should go straight ahead on one's own path of *sadhana*. One who wastes his time in finding fault with or abusing other paths is indeed a stupid and unfortunate creature. Such an ignorant person is not entitled to have the vision of God. He invites and causes not only his own decline, but probably that of others. Genuine aspirants should beware of such pitfalls. God is one for all.

Bhagavan Nityananda used to say that it is the same power which has manifested itself as Ram or Rahim, Keshav or Karim, and again it is the same power which has manifested itself as Christ, Allah, Madhava, or Mahadeva. The Puranas, the Koran, and the Bible all speak of Him alone. The ultimate goal implied in the teachings of all books of religion is the same. Only those who have faulty conceptions and whose *tapasya* (practice of spiritual austerities) is not pure and perfect think in terms of superior and inferior and create confusion. In fact, for all beings the earth is one and the sky is one, and similarly the air they breathe, the water they drink, and the food they eat is the same. Even the sustaining life force and the all-pervading *chaitanya* are the same. The nature of joy that is felt in the heart is also one for all living beings. Where, then, lies the difference? Can a person who sees and preaches distinctions be considered a religious being?

By its very nature, the Godhead is supremely blissful. It is full of love and sees no differences whatsoever. To commit the crime of making the distinctions of mine and yours, superior and inferior, is not the way to worship God. On the contrary, it is love of God that develops complete peace, everlasting peace, and nothing but peace. A person turns to religion so that he can have true inner peace. The peace that the ancient sages attained within their innermost selves is attainable not only by Hindus, but equally by the followers of the Bible and the Koran. This is because the peace which spontaneously rises in the heart is essentially the same for all. He who resides in everyone's heart is full of peace, bliss, love, and wisdom and is effulgent and omnipresent. He is that most subtle Absolute Truth, the adorable God of all beings, and That alone is *satchidananda*, or the Godhead.

SATCHIDANANDA

Let us now try to understand the meaning of the word *satchidananda*, which is the true nature of God as realized by the sages, the knowers of Truth.

The term *sat* indicates that which exists in equal proportion in all beings, at all times, and in all places. The *atman* pervades everything in full measure and is the support of all. Every visible object therefore rests in the *sat* aspect of God. Nothing exists without a support. Houses, factories, temples, mosques, and all other buildings are supported by the earth. Gold is the basis for all golden ornaments. Cotton thread forms the warp and woof of different types of cotton cloth. In the same way, God is the basic essence of which the entire universe is made. In other words, God is the fundamental fiber from which the entire pattern of the universe springs. That is why God is *sat*, real existence, and is the moving force behind the process of creation, sustenance, and dissolution of the universe. He is everything. He is Reality itself, and therefore Truth is His very nature. A seeker of Truth therefore attains God.

The second aspect of God is *chit*, which means cosmic intelligence or knowledge. *Chit* is also called Chiti, the Universal Consciousness. Chiti is that which at all times and in all places manifests or discloses everything as it is. Like the candlelight which makes things visible in the dark, *chit* reveals whether or not an object exists. *Chit*, which imparts life or consciousness to all and shines forth through all objects, is Chiti itself. The vision of the eyes, the hearing of the ears, and the power of speech are all the functions of that very *atman* which is Consciousness. This power is known as Chiti because it is the light of the sun and the moon and the effulgence of fire. It is the light of all lights in the universe. This very Chiti shines in the form of a divine, lustrous flame in everyone's heart, forehead, and *sahasrara.* Fortunate *sadhakas* see this light during meditation by the grace of the Guru. However, even when it becomes visible, it is not different from the Absolute Brahman, which has no form or attributes.

This Chiti is the sovereign power governing all life, and hence it cannot be the exclusive possession of any particular sect or creed. Just as, according to Vedanta, this world is an imagination of the mind superimposed on the *atman,* so are all the different faiths of the world creations of the mind, yet not separate from Chiti. Only pure Chiti (cleansed of all impurities and ignorance) can enter or be admitted into the greater Universal Chiti. Just as a river loses its name and identity when it merges into the vast ocean, so is an individual admitted into the realm of infinite wisdom when all his man-made cults and creeds cease to exist. In that supreme wisdom, all imaginary beliefs and faiths melt away and the vanity of their followers also evaporates. To Chiti, the entire world is its own manifestation. In its realm there is no inequality; only for people who have not been fortunate enough to receive the grace of the Guru does inequality exist. How could the Chidrupa Paramatman (Lord of wisdom) ever distinguish between Ram and Rahim, or Christ and Krishna, when such differences do not exist for those who have realized the Truth by His grace? It is Chiti that pervades the entire conscious manifestation. One who realizes Chiti perceives the entire world and all the different religions as existing in that Chiti, and nothing else. To say that the entire world is the manifestation of *chidatman*, the all-knowing Self, is the same as saying that the entire world is Chiti itself.

The third aspect of God is *ananda*, that is, joy or bliss. The *Taittiriya Upanishad* (III, 6) says that Brahman is bliss. All things are born out of bliss, are maintained by bliss, and ultimately merge into bliss. The Vedas and other scriptures, the seers, the sages, and all the enlightened ones unanimously affirm that bliss itself is the Supreme Lord. In fact, every activity in our life is motivated either to express joy or to acquire joy. A child is born out of happiness. We develop and sustain mutual relations with a view to becoming happy. Our striving for progress is also meant to bring more happiness. We undertake all our activities and fulfill all our duties not to create more sects and dogmas, more paths and divisions, but rather to experience more bliss and happiness in life. Why does a human being seek joy in everything? It is because the very nature of the Self is *ananda*, or bliss.

Just as *sat* pervades everywhere, so also *chit* fills everything in full measure. *Sat* is *chit*, and *chit* is *ananda*. Therefore, *ananda* too fills everything fully. All our mutual relations are based on love. Is not a mother's love for her child pure and selfless? Do we not find older people loving younger ones just for the sake of love? The sweet smile of a child playing merrily in the lap of its mother, a husband's love for his wife or the unreserved sacrifice of a wife's entire life for the love of her husband, the willingness of a disciple to surrender everything unconditionally at the feet of his Guru, and the grace with which the Guru bestows on the disciple the gift of his own inner bliss, which makes him dance in ecstasy and awakens him from the evil dream of imaginary grief—all these support the view that the soul, which is born out of bliss, is bliss itself.

Tender shoots of corn grow merrily into ears of corn; new foliage blooms and beautiful flowers blossom; the sun and moon rise and set regularly, playing in their own delight; the galaxies of stars and constellations twinkle and illuminate the sky; the wind dances in all directions, drunk with its own joy, blowing its own music into every home; and the rippling waters of rivers and rivulets flow continuously, singing the name of the Lord; a person in distress is consoled by the kind words of a happy soul; the holy waters of the Ganges gladly wash away all impurities and sins, and bring peace and piety; Mother Earth cheerfully bears the burden of the entire world and offers fresh, ever-new harvests of infinite variety out of the fullness of her deep love; the cuckoo sings sweet melodies; and the *chataka* bird gives out its cries of love. Why are they all so happy? It is because they are born out of Brahman, whose very nature is joy and bliss. Bliss is the Supreme Lord. And all the Upanishads declare that the Supreme Lord is *satchidananda*.

JIVATMAN

Vedanta philosophy declares that *jiva*, the individual, and Brahman, the Absolute, are one. It is true that the *jivatman* (individual soul) is the same as Paramatman (the Supreme Self). The Supreme Self projects itself in the form of individual selves and again merges into its original Self. The Lord declares in the *Bhagavad Gita* (XV, 7) that all individual selves are part of the Lord's own eternal Spirit, *mamaivāmsho jīvaloke jīvabhūtah sanātanah*, for none other than the Lord can become a *jivatman*. The *Taittiriya Upanishad* (II,6) says, *tat srushtvā tadevānuprāvishat*—"Having created it, He Himself entered into it." Having created the physical bodies of all creatures, Paramatman Himself entered into them to make them alive and active. Is it the fleshy human mechanism that can make the eyes see or the tongue speak, that gives the power of hearing to the ears or the power of smell to the nose? Does the flesh have the power to see anything? No. It is Consciousness—the soul—residing and vibrating in the inner sanctum of the human temple which makes the senses function. The *atman* is absolutely pure, perfect, and changeless. It is so pure that none of the good or bad qualities of the physical body can affect it.

The *atman* exists in infinite physical bodies and yet remains untouched by them. It may seem to be tainted by the impurities of the mind, but if one follows yoga practices as instructed by the Guru, the mind and senses are purified of all thoughts and desires. Then the *antahkarana* (inner being) becomes extremely subtle. Such a perfectly pure *antahkarana* is by all means ready to receive and experience divine bliss. It is indeed possible, at that stage, to attain realization of the ever-pure inner Self.

Jivatman, by its very nature, is pure, divine luster. Saint Kabir said:

> *saba ghata sāī rame hai,*
> *sūnī seja nā koī.*

> God dwells in everybody; not even one form is left out.

In the *Bhagavad Gita* (XVIII, 61), the Lord tells Arjuna that God dwells in the heart of every being: *īshvarah sarvabhūtānām hruddeshe'rjuna tishthati.* Bhagavan Shri Nityananda used to tell the same thing to *sadhakas:* "God is within you. Why are you searching for Him in jungles? Why all these unnecessary wanderings?" In the *Sadachar,* Shankaracharya says:

> *deho devālayah prokto,*
> *dehī devo niranjanah.*

> The body is spoken of as the temple, and the indwelling soul as the immaculate God.

In other words, the human body is a holy temple, and the *jivatman* that dwells within is none other than Paramatman. This identity of *jivatman* and Paramatman is realized when the state of *So'ham* ("I am That") is actually experienced after complete purification of the mind. But this realization becomes possible only when the Sadguru bestows his grace upon the disciple. As the wise say, the indwelling soul is concealed by a thin but tough veil of ignorance, which does not allow us to know the purity and perfection of that soul. This ignorance is burned up in the fire of yoga, which is kindled by the grace of the Guru through *shaktipat*. The individual soul then truly realizes its identity with the Supreme Self and is inspired to repeat *Shivo'ham* ("I am Shiva"), the greatest of all mantras.

This *jivatman* clings to its limited individuality only so long as it does not realize its true Self. This is an imaginary bondage which makes the soul think of itself as imperfect. The *Pratyabhijnahridayam* says:

ayam shaktidaridraha samsārī uchyate.

One who has become poor in Shakti is called a transmigratory being.

In other words, a soul that has no knowledge of the true nature of the Self and has remained unenlightened because of its failure to earn the grace of the Guru, considering itself to be only a flesh-and-blood body, is unhappy and aware of duality because of its ignorance. But as the *Pratyabhijnahridayam* further says:

svashaktivikāse tu shiva eva.

With the unfolding of his inherent Shakti, however, one is Lord Shiva Himself.

In other words, one who has searched within, who has studied Vedanta philosophy well, who has practiced yoga and meditation, whose ego is completely annihilated, and who is devout, pious, and unattached, sees God within himself by the grace of the Guru. When the disciple's latent Shakti unfolds itself fully by the Guru's blessings, the feeling of "I am *jiva*" (*jivo'ham*) vanishes, and the knowledge that "I am Shiva" (*Shivo'ham*) dawns. That blessed soul then permanently lives in the awareness of "I am Shiva." This is like an ordinary soldier becoming a king because of some past merit, never again to revert to his former position.

Lord Krishna says in the *Bhagavad Gita* (IV, 37):

jñānāgnih sarvakarmāni bhasmasātkurute tathā.

The fire of knowledge burns all *karmas* to ashes.

When, through the grace of the Guru, the divine spark of knowledge burns up the veil of ignorance, the disciple has a direct glimpse of the true nature of his Self and is enraptured by the pure bliss of the Self (*atmananda*). This is fulfillment or beatitude, which is the same as enlightenment or Self-realization.

3

Guru and Disciple

The many different powers we see in this world are nothing but different manifestations of God. Among these, the Guru is the most glorious manifestation of that Supreme Self, and so the Guru is known as the very embodiment of Supreme Reality: *guruh sākshātparabrahma*. The greatness of the Guru is described in the *Shiva Sutra Vimarshini:*

> *gururvā pārameshvarī anugrāhikā shaktihi.*

The Guru is the grace-bestowing power of the Supreme Lord.

In India all those who have been known for their achievements became great only by their Guru's blessings. The greatness and glory of Kabir Sahib, Jnaneshvar Maharaj, and Shri Ekanath Maharaj originated from the gift of the blessings of their Guru. The Guru is therefore called *kalpa-vruksha*, the celestial tree, which fulfills every desire. The fortunate one who is blessed by the Guru's grace transcends human limitations and attains divinity.

As we understand the nature of the Guru more and more, we come to realize that the Guru is the embodiment of all gods, the essence of all that is holy, and the power which awards the fruit of all good deeds. One who seeks refuge at the feet of the Guru creates a heaven for himself and lives happily.

A real Guru is one who is well-versed in the holy scriptures, has identified himself completely with the Supreme
Self, is capable of dispelling every doubt from a disciple's
mind by convincing him thoroughly of the Truth, and can
give the direct experience of Self-realization to a worthy
disciple. The Guru's greatness, therefore, is infinite.

One who guides aspirants on the divine path is called a
Guru. Teachers are held in high respect not only in India
but in countries all over the world. The greatness of one
who can transmit the divine power of his own soul to a
disciple is beyond words. The divine gifts of the Guru are
incalculable.

The Guru's consciousness remains permanently one with
that of the Universal Self. That is why the Guru is
everywhere, even when he appears to be present at one
place. He is looked upon as a manifestation of Supreme
Reality because he is the knower of the highest Truth and
is firmly established in it, having achieved the direct experience of the Divine.

The Guru is not bound by the distinctions of any particular class or order of life. He is far beyond the formalities of
religious or worldly duties since he has become one with
the Supreme Self, which is the source of all purity. Body-
consciousness cannot remain alive after the final realization. Such an individual remains steady in the experience
that everything abides in him because he is the embodiment of pure Consciousness, the indivisible Brahman.

Intense devotion for and service to such a Sadguru indeed results in the divine attainment, which is the highest
reward of all spiritual endeavor.

> sachchidbrahma guruh sākshāt
> pūjyam sevyam aharnisham;
> rāmakrishnādidevānām
> sadguru brahma tārakam.

The Guru, who is the visible form of *sat*, *chit*, and
Brahman, should be worshipped and served day and

night. Even Rama and Krishna received enlightenment through the Sadguru.

The Guru possesses superhuman powers, and that is why
even divine beings like Lord Rama and Lord Krishna
showed that one can obtain Self-knowledge by surrender at
the feet of the Guru. We may be inclined to treat this as
mythological legend, but we should remember that in the
recent past a young, educated atheist named Narendra was
completely convinced of the divine power of the Guru by
accepting Shri Ramakrishna Paramahansa as his Guru, and
obtaining his grace through diligent service. He became
famous as Swami Vivekananda, who is held in high esteem
by the entire world.

In fact, the Guru is the soul of everything. The world is
the manifestation of the Guru, and the Guru is the world in
essence. The entire world, with all its movable and immovable contents, is the Guru. The Universal Consciousness,
which is the cause and the basis of all creation, is itself the
Guru. That same Guru is the power of action in the animate world. He is also the power of knowledge in all living
beings, and it is he who works as the supreme willpower.

After awakening the spiritual force in a disciple, the
Guru becomes its protector and controller. It is the Guru
who manifests himself in the form of divine power in the
heart of deserving disciples. It is the Guru who shines forth
in and through the disciple, just as it is the father who is
born in the son.

There are many types of gurus, but only one who is
well-versed in all scriptures, and who is capable of making a
disciple attain the highest bliss by destroying his limited
individuality and making him experience his identity with
the Supreme Self through *shaktipat,* is worthy of the highest
adoration.

The more profound our reverence and regard for the
Guru, the deeper and firmer our spiritual progress becomes.
A story from the *Chandogya Upanishad* narrates how, under

orders from the Guru, all the elements appeared in person
and explained their secrets to a disciple called Satyakam
Jabala, who diligently obeyed the Guru's instructions.
Jabala was asked by his Guru to tend four hundred cows in
the jungle and return only when they had multiplied to one
thousand. Obeying his Guru's command, Jabala took the
cows to the jungle and looked after them with utmost care
while he himself subsisted on what the jungle could give
him in the form of roots and fruits. He constantly remem-
bered his Guru and performed his duty with an unwavering
mind, even in the most trying circumstances. After some
years, when the number of cows had finally increased to
one thousand, Jabala prepared to return to his Guru. The
very thought of meeting the Guru in person and having the
holy *darshan* of his sacred feet made his heart overflow with
joy. While he was on his way, the five elements of the
universe, pleased at his single-minded devotion to the
Guru, manifested themselves before him one by one and
revealed the secret and essence of their working.

Even the worship of the Guru's clay image brings these
results, as the story of Eklavya from the great epic, the
Mahabharata, illustrates. Eklavya came from a backward tri-
bal family, and so Dronacharya, the Guru of the royal
princes, refused to teach him archery, thinking that it
might be misused. Eklavya was, however, determined to
learn the science and had unflinching faith in the power of
the Guru. He therefore made a clay image of Dronacharya
and started worshipping it. By constant meditation and repetition of the Guru's holy name, his entire being became
one with the Guru. Through such deep contemplation, the
Guru's power spontaneously shone in his heart and imparted full knowledge of the science of archery to him. He
automatically learned all that Dronacharya knew. He even
learned the great secrets which Dronacharya himself had
not taught to anyone. If so much power could be invoked
even in a clay image of the Guru, could anything be impos-

sible to achieve by praying, serving, and worshipping the Guru himself, who is the living embodiment of Brahman, the Supreme Reality?

There is also the story of Giri, an illiterate *brahmin* boy who became highly proficient in Vedanta merely by his rare devotion to Shri Shankaracharya, whom he had accepted as his Guru. He was a simple and devoted soul who fully believed that service to the Guru was the source of all knowledge. He therefore devoted himself faithfully to the service of the Acharya. He never neglected his duties and was always quick to perform every possible service to the Guru. Whenever the Acharya taught Vedanta to his pupils, Giri would very humbly stand by and listen. One day the Acharya held the class as usual but would not start the lesson. When the pupils asked him if he was waiting for someone, the Acharya replied that he was waiting for Giri. The pupils laughed and said, "Gurudev! Giri has gone to the river to wash your clothes. You may begin the lessons. It doesn't matter whether Giri is present or not since he doesn't understand or grasp anything."

This callousness pained Shankaracharya. In order to emphasize the value of *gurubhakti* (devotion to the Guru) and remove the pupils' false pride in intelligence and book-learning, he taught them not to belittle an illiterate, but devout *sadhaka*. By his mere wish, he transmitted his grace to Giri. Instantly, the boy was inspired to compose Sanskrit verses in praise of the Guru, and with the Guru's clothes in his hands, he returned and stood before Shankaracharya, reciting the verses with humility. All the pupils were surprised by this miraculous change in Giri and at once realized their mistake. Giri thus became an enlightened soul by the grace of the Guru and became well-known as Totakacharya. This is the greatness and power of *gurubhakti*. Let us now look at the qualities of a true disciple and the nature of his devotion to the Guru.

A TRUE DISCIPLE

Discrimination *(viveka)* and nonattachment *(vairagya)* are the two main qualifications of one who wishes to be a disciple.

The ancient seers described mundane existence as dry, insipid, deceptive, ephemeral, and filled with suffering. Even Lord Krishna says in the *Bhagavad Gita* (IX, 33) that this world is fleeting and full of unhappiness: *anityam-asukham lokamimam.* One poet sings:

> *aba to gāfil jāga re . . .*
> *dekhate murajhāya jāya kyā karatā hai rāga re,*
> *jāga re nara jāga re.*
> *māyā-jāla bichhāyā hai, lambe isase bhāga re,*
> *jāga re nara jāga re.*

> Wake up at least now, O careless one. Why waste your love on a world that is transient? O man, wake up; oh, wake up. Flee from this illusive net of *maya.* O man, wake up; oh, wake up.

A person's suffering starts from the moment he is conceived. After a long, miserable confinement in his mother's womb, he is finally born as a helpless baby, entirely dependent on others. As a youth he is plagued by all sorts of temptations and greed, and as an adult he is burned in the fire of lust and worldly desires. Finally, he reaches old age with all its infirmities, ugliness, fears, and helplessness. Where is the pleasure then? The truth is that an individual soul is born in this world to reap the fruits of its many good and bad past deeds. It lives for a while, dies, and is born again; thus, the cycle of birth and death goes on. Where are all the great kings and mighty warriors who once ruled this earth? Where have they all gone? The world we see is transitory and ever changing. That alone is true and real which is eternally free and changeless, not bound by the limits of time, space, and causation. The *atman* is true, pure, perfect, immortal, tranquil, and beautiful. Anything other than the *atman* is not real, for it changes and perishes with the passage of time. From time immemorial, there have been innumerable great beings. Where are they now? Just as the past has not survived, so the present order will also perish in the future. One who has this understanding and can discriminate between the eternal and the transient is fit for initiation on the divine path. Such a person has a genuine desire to realize the true nature of human beings, God, and the world, as well as to know the significance of yoga, *bhakti,* and *jnana.* Therefore, he honestly follows the path shown by the Guru and is indeed a blessed seeker.

A true disciple is one who merges his entire individuality into his Guru. Such a disciple himself becomes a Guru in course of time. In fact, a true devotee is one who has merged his identity with God; a perfect yogi is one who is always in communion with the inner Self; and, likewise, a true disciple is one whose soul is forever united with the Guru.

In the *Gita* (XVIII, 73) Arjuna says to Lord Krishna, *karishye vachanam tava*—"I will do Thy bidding." We can therefore say that one who has complete faith in the Guru's words and lives in complete accord with his wishes is a true disciple. Jnaneshvar Maharaj says that the words of the Guru purify the mind: *guruvachani mana dhutale.* Such a disciple inherits a great spiritual legacy and in due time attains the position of Guru. An ideal disciple is studious, attentive, alert, practical, and dutiful and has complete faith in the Guru's teachings. A disciple perfect in *gurubhakti* breaks the bondage of worldly existence, cuts the tie of delusion, and burns the net of obstacles through the strength of his devotion, dispassion, and discrimination. He is not carried away by the river of illusions nor parched by the fire of sufferings and sorrow. He is afraid of no one, nor does he frighten anyone; he is neither a coward nor a tyrant.

The subject of discipleship is very difficult to understand, and its secrets are beyond the conception of most people. There is hardly anything to match the greatness of a *sadhaka* who qualifies for discipleship by purifying his mind thoroughly. There are many teachers in the world, but illustrious disciples, such as Jabala, Eklavya, Totakacharya, Gavba, and Vivekananda, are rare. Just as Eklavya, though born in a low caste, became a master archer by his single-minded devotion to his Guru Dronacharya, so also Gavba, an illiterate disciple of Ekanath Maharaj of Paithan, completed the unfinished *Bhavartha Ramayana* of his Guru. Gavba was the son of a poor widow. He was very fond of sweets, particularly *puran poli* (sweet flat breads), which his poor mother could not afford. One day, the mother lost all her patience and took the boy to Ekanath Maharaj, whose fame had spread far and wide. Ekanath Maharaj was moved by the mother's plight and asked the boy if he would stay with him if he got *puran poli* every day. The boy agreed to stay. Because of his excessive love for *puran poli*, he was nicknamed Puranpolya. He never learned anything and was considered foolish and crazy. He was, however, extremely devoted to Shri Ekanath and willingly did all the work that was allotted to him. He worshipped Ekanath. He meditated on Ekanath. He worked for Ekanath. For him, Ekanath was everything that mattered. At this time, Ekanath Maharaj was nearing his *mahasamadhi* (a yogi's final, conscious exit from the body), and one of his great works, the *Bhavartha Ramayana*, was likely to remain incomplete if the saint passed away. All of the devotees were worried, but Shri Ekanath allayed their fears, and also surprised them, by declaring that his work would be completed by the illiterate Gavba. He then placed his hand on Gavba's head and infused him with the very spirit of his own inspiration. This transformed Gavba into an inspired soul, and the verses he composed thereafter are not distinguishable from those composed earlier by Shri Ekanath Maharaj himself. The grace of the Guru and the devotion of the disciple thus elevated the disciple to the position of the Guru.

The ancient sages expounded various means—such as austerity, penance, repetition of the divine name, charity, religious vows, fasting, pilgrimages, image worship, and meditation on the Formless—for acquiring fame and fortune and becoming pure and noble. They are, no doubt, true and rewarding. Even so, for a genuine *sadhaka,* a seeker of the highest Truth, Shishya Yoga—that is, accepting discipleship under a Sadguru and proceeding on the spiritual path according to his teachings, instructions, and guidance—is the best. Shishya Yoga, the path of discipleship, is great in every respect.

Today there are swamis, philosophers, and lecturers on religious subjects who openly refute the tradition of discipleship and, by so doing, automatically eliminate the sacred tradition of the Guru. Such people not only blindly follow the wrong path under some delusion, but also lead others into the wilderness. There are also book-learned scholars, so-called *jnanis* devoid of any direct experience of the Divine, people with hearts completely lacking in the warmth of devotion, and similar insipid types who pose as spiritual guides. There are some self-styled teachers as well who have neither learned the basic techniques of yoga, nor acquainted themselves with the direct inner experience of wisdom through any Guru, but who still assume the position of Guru and start guiding others. Can a person who has not accepted anyone's discipleship, who has not obtained any knowledge from a Guru, be the guide or the Guru of others? What can a pauper give in charity? How can an illiterate person teach, or a blind man lead? What is there to give if one has not received? Such people give discourses on philosophy, guide their listeners, and, strangely enough, simultaneously denounce the sacred tradition of the Guru. Could there be a greater paradox?

What is discipleship? Discipleship, the acceptance of a Guru, implies unconditional surrender at the feet of the

Guru. The underlying idea is difficult to comprehend. To be a disciple is to belong to the Guru wholeheartedly through love, devotion, faith, meditation, understanding, and direct spiritual experiences. Just as a droplet of water becomes the ocean by merging with it, so also does the disciple become identical with the Guru within a short time by uniting himself with the Guru in his own heart through pure love and devotion.

The scriptures speak of two types of sons: one is known as *viryajata,* and the other as *mantrajata.* A *viryajata* son is born from the father's semen, while one who is initiated by a Guru through *shaktipat* and mantra *diksha* is the Guru's *mantrajata* son. In fact, spiritually, the latter relationship is more real than the former. The Guru transmits into the disciple his lustrous *mantravirya,* which is potent with the power of penance, yoga, and *jnana.* The *mantravirya* is the very essence of supreme knowledge, and it transforms the disciple into a wonderful new being, full of the burning fire of yoga. In other words, the Guru transforms the disciple into his own prototype; then the disciple becomes identical with the Guru.

How does a disciple attain oneness with the Guru? He becomes one with the Guru by subduing the ego and merging himself completely into the Guru through every thought, word, and deed. By constant contemplation of the idea that the Self is the Guru and the Guru is Parashiva, the supremely benevolent Godhead, the disciple attains perfect, indivisible union with him. Such a one is indeed a true disciple.

A disciple who surrenders totally, without holding anything back, becomes the very image of the Guru through constant reflection and unceasing meditation upon the Guru. This is like the transformation of a larva into a wasp by the larva's contact with the wasp. Such a disciple is indeed true and great.

Many people ask why all the disciples of the same Guru do not make uniform spiritual progress or turn out to be exactly the same. This is because of the difference in their standards and abilities. All are not equally worthy or virtuous, and therefore, even though several disciples may be initiated by the same Guru, in one the divine Shakti may develop and shine fully, in another it may show only partial development, while in a third it may not show any visible effects at all.

After having experienced the spiritual greatness of the Guru, a true disciple does not raise doubts about the Guru's way of life, behavior, dealings, or method of teaching. Such scepticism obstructs a disciple's march toward spiritual perfection and attainment of Guruhood. One who tries to find fault with Gurus and thinks that they, like other human beings, are governed by passions such as anger or hatred does not deserve to be called a disciple. Discipleship implies complete dedication to the Guru and thus getting in return everything that the Guru can give. One who gives in full gets back in full. If a disciple holds something back, he gets that much less in return from the Guru. If, by the will of God, a Guru is hallowed with glory, surrounded by wealth, honored by the world, or happens to possess mystical powers or estates or ashrams, any number of people will rush to become his disciples with intentions all too apparent. But these are only wealth worshippers and bargain hunters. They are not true disciples fit to take the Guru's place of honor.

A disciple must be devoted to the Guru. A disciple's devotion is nothing but his selfless love for the Guru. *Bhakti* means love, and *gurubhakti* implies harnessing one's mind, body, and soul entirely in the service of the Guru, implicit obedience to the Guru, continuous remembrance of the Guru, and selfless love for the Guru. These qualities combined make a true disciple. Such a one is blessed by the gods. To him, all mantras bear fruit and all *siddhis* (mystical powers) easily accrue. If such a disciple happens to be a householder, he can easily realize God in the very midst of his family life; he does not have to leave his home in search of God. If, on the other hand, he has already renounced the material world, he very easily attains the state of Self-realization, which is the fulfillment of all desires.

A true disciple continues to be a disciple and retains the spirit of diligent service to the Guru even after attaining the highest state of yoga—the state of Self-realization—when he becomes an adept in *shaktipat*.

A river of bliss flows through this divine union of the Guru and the disciple, in which countless people bathe to be purified and become holy.

4

The Nectar of Love
for the Guru

Love is *bhakti,* and *bhakti* means love. The awakening of deep and boundless affection for one's beloved Guru is love of Self, or *bhakti* (devotion). Such devotion is of the highest order and does not depend on formalities such as yogic practices, worship, rituals, or study. When the mind is desireless, when worldly objects do not attract it, when the wish for heavenly happiness and even the desire for salvation vanish and with full affection the mind is firmly established in the lotus feet of Shri Gurudev, that state of the highest, all-exclusive love is known as *bhakti.* Such *bhakti,* such supreme love, is ambrosial in its very essence. To love only Shri Gurudev with all the intensity of the heart is real *amrit* (nectar). This *amrit* is the sweetest of all. One who receives and drinks it becomes immortal. Worldly desire is death.

An unwavering *bhakta* (devotee) always longs for the ever-fresh and pure love of his Guru. No other desire remains in his heart. He longs only for Shri Gurudev. Such a *bhakta* will see the divine form of his Gurudev, hear the sweet name of his beloved Guru, and utter softly the name "Shri Gurudev." His worldly life of give and take is filled with his Guru. In short, his only longing is for the lotus feet of the Sadguru.

When such a rare longing arises by Shri Gurudev's grace, the devotee, taking full advantage of this state of blissfulness which even the sages crave, becomes free from the cycle of birth and death. His heart then becomes Gurudev's temple. The union between an ardent devotee and the beloved Guru is in itself immortality. This culmination is the height of *gurubhakti*.

A devotee who has drunk *guru-premamrit* (the nectar of love for the beloved Guru) has truly reached perfection. The power of this perfect state is incomparable and beyond the miraculous *ashtasiddhis* (the eight supernatural powers). A true devotee does not want these *siddhis*. When the real, the perfect, the source-of-all is achieved, the mind does not run after inferior and incomplete *siddhis*; the devotee does not even wish for salvation. Having reached the region of complete bliss, he is thoroughly satiated. Such a state of fulfillment and supreme joy, which is not easily attained even by gods and Siddhas, is enjoyed by the devotee on the strength of his devotion to the Guru, his Master. His worldly desires are extinguished by this fulfillment. He realizes that prosperity, beauty, sweetness, love, power, fame, and even knowledge and renunciation, which people always crave, are worthless compared to the rare love of a delighted soul. If one collects all the objects of the three worlds, they will not give the happiness equal to the supreme bliss which even a drop from the ocean of *nityananda* (eternal bliss) will give.

In gain or loss, praise or insult, the devotee always remains cheerful. If he can gain the Guru's love and grace, the devotee, who has devoted his all to the service of the Master, does not care even if some obstacle comes in his way to salvation. His only earnest desire is that his love for the Guru will always increase. Being pleased and attracted by this love and devotion, God Himself showers joy-giving *amrit* in the devotee's heart. What could be more valuable than that love? Such a blessed devotee then lives perpetually in a state of blissful intoxication.

All the doubts of a devotee who has attained the nectar
of knowledge from Shri Guru melt away. Knowing that the
world around him is the *lila* (sport) of his beloved Guru, he
becomes free of illusions. He can go where he likes. His
Gurudev appears to fill the entire world. Is there a place
where Shri Gurudev does not exist? Which object is not
pervaded by Shri Guru? Gurudev is the source of all animate beings as well as inanimate objects of this world. The
devotee knows that the entire universe is one with Shri
Guru. The basic support of the universe is the superconscious soul of Shri Guru alone. That which the Vedas describe after endless search as "not this, not this," which is
even beyond the primordial sound *Omkar*, which is the root
of all forms, and in which this complete universe exists —
that eternal, unknown, indestructible Principle is beloved
Shri Gurudev. He is the root of all religions — self-existent,
immutable, and the ruler of the universe.

Having come to know the all-pervasiveness of the Master, the devotee may stay anywhere and still devote himself
to his Gurudev. He can sing the prayers of love and devotion which are inspired by his heart. Such a devotee considers time, place, past, present, here, and there to be in-
separable from Shri Guru. Just as the air molds itself in any
form and moves everywhere, this devotee, being enlightened with the knowledge of the Self, joyfully moves in
all three worlds.

To see and realize Shri Gurudev in all living beings is
real devotion. This love for all comes through Shri Guru's
grace and makes the devotee almost mad. Intoxicated with
love, he goes on singing the praises of the Master day and
night. He hears, speaks, sings, and thinks of Shri Guru
alone. Like a drunkard or a lunatic, he acts and talks in a
manner which seems senseless. He remains absorbed in a
state of intoxication with Guru's love. His heart melts with
extreme love and adoration for the Guru, and when this
state reaches its peak, the ecstatic devotee may sometimes

laugh heartily, cry, shout, sing loudly, or even dance. In
this sublime state, he experiences oneness with Shri Guru.
His mind and body become calm and peaceful.

Life then becomes joyful and worthwhile for such a devotee. He alone is an *atmaram* (one who is absorbed in the
Self). Because everything is merged into Shri Guru, no ideas
of distinction or duality, love and hate, mine and yours,
small and great remain in him. This is oneness in love, a
state of absolute nonduality attained through love. When
the devotee is thus established in oneness with Shri Guru,
his separate existence disappears altogether. The secret of
achieving this unique state of love is abandoning the desire
for worldly objects. Not only does the longing for money,
husband or wife, children, fame, and heaven vanish, but in
this intoxicated state not even the desire for liberation sur-
vives. The devotion which asks or hopes for something in
return is a sort of selfish bargain filled with ambition.

In the *Bhagavad Gita* Lord Krishna says:

> *ye hi samsparshajā bhogā duhkhayonaya eva te;*
> *ādyantavantah kaunteya na teshu ramate budhah.*

> O son of Kunti, the joys derived from sensual con-
> tacts are the source of misery; they have a begin-
> ning and an end. The wise person does not delight
> therein.

It is a fact that the pleasure derived through the senses is
not real happiness. It brings only misery in its wake. One
who has earned the sweet love of his Guru is really happy.
One who fails to obtain this love is allured by the senses
and becomes entangled in sensual pleasures. Just as a starv-
ing man gulps down mud or sand, or a deer oppressed by
thirst mistakes a mirage for real water and runs after it
only to meet death, those who do not realize the worth of
Shri Guru's love and are deluded by sensual enjoyments,
lust, and wealth meet poverty and misery in the false
name of happiness. A wise person who has completely

freed his body and mind from impure tendencies by the constant remembrance and repetition of Shri Gurudev's name becomes pure.* His thoughts of likes and dislikes are easily destroyed. Where is there room for duality in the devotee's heart when the supreme bliss of Absolute Reality resides in all its grandeur? By experiencing eternal joy within himself, the devotee attains a state of Self-absorption which removes his entire ego. When ego and pride thus disappear, the individual soul, merging in the sweet love of the Guru, so closely embraces him that at that very moment, like the mingling of a wave with the ocean, the soul of the individual becomes united with that of his Guru to become indivisibly one. When one looks at air in the sky, it is difficult to determine which is air and which is sky. Likewise, when the devotee and the Guru become spiritually united, all distinctions and inequalities are destroyed and only the essence, *nityananda*, remains as the devotee's true Self. Differences having come to an end, only an unbroken flow of supreme joy remains. The *gurubhakta* then looks like the embodiment of joy. Renunciation of all desires is easily attained through intense love.

There is a natural flow of love in the heart of every individual. This is because each soul, being a part of the Absolute Reality, naturally possesses its essential qualities of intense joy and supreme love. But the stream of love is contaminated by its contact with sense objects. Hence, that pure love turns into passions, which bring endless miseries. As a result of these impurities in the stream of love, one cannot perceive the divine light of the Supreme shining within oneself. In order to enjoy the delightful supreme love and divine light, it is essential to change the course of the mind, which runs after earthly pleasures, and make it introspective. The mind can be bent in any direction. Unless it completely leaves the muddy pool of sen-

---

*Here, "Shri Gurudev's name" refers to the mantra given by the Guru.

sual objects, it cannot enjoy a swim in the ocean of eternal bliss. It is impossible to sing a song and chew hard nuts at the same time. After tasting nectar, who would relish sense delights?

Prayer is the only thing which gives rise to love in one's heart. One experiences nectar-like love for Shri Guru by constant repetition of and meditation on his name. Thus, devotional prayer is both a means and an end in itself. For one who has earned love for Shri Gurudev, meditation naturally becomes a continuous phenomenon. Hence, whoever wants to achieve love for Shri Gurudev should repeat his name unceasingly. A person who desires liberation without earning it with prayer, devotion, meditation, and renunciation is committing a grave mistake. He is deceiving himself. He is like one who cuts his own feet with an axe. After many years of constant meditation on Shri Gurudev and by repetition of his name with all sincerity and respect, love and devotion will arise in one's heart. In other words, it is absolutely necessary to learn and master the means to this end.

A devotee or spiritual aspirant should always avoid evil association. Bad company slowly gives rise to low tendencies, bad habits, and evil instincts. Furthermore, it destroys all the ennobling qualities inherent in human beings, and then all calamities follow. By listening to the ill advice of her maid Manthara, Queen Kaikeyi, who was a very loving, affectionate, and noble lady, became the cause of extreme grief and sorrow to King Dasharatha and all the people of Ayodhya. As a result, she became a widow and lost all the love and respect of her dear son, Bharata. Association with the evil-minded Shakuni is considered the prime cause of the battle in the *Mahabharata*, which brought about terrible ruin and destruction. Therefore, one who wants happiness should stay away from all vices and wickedness.

God, love, delight, supreme happiness, absolute joy, and eternal bliss are just different names for that one Supreme

Reality and knowledge. It is impossible to define Brahman. Even the Vedas remain silent after describing it as "not this, not this." Similarly, one cannot describe the sweetness of love for Shri Guru. Even in worldly life, the inner joy one experiences on meeting one's beloved, or on receiving news of one's sweetheart, is beyond expression. That which one puts in words is only the outer form of love. Actually love is to be felt, experienced, tasted. One who is fully immersed in the ocean of love is unable to utter anything, like a dumb person who only smiles when he tastes a lump of sugar but cannot speak about its sweetness. This is because there is no language which can explain divine love. When the heart is filled with that supreme joy, all outer consciousness is lost and one becomes silent.

This love is without any qualifications or desires. It grows every moment and is finer than the finest form of experience. It is nothing but the blissful soul of the Lord Shri Guru residing in the secret alcove of one's heart. This love is the highest joy. Being immersed in such divine *rasa* (that which is most relishable) of supreme delight, the blessed devotee is unable to see anything but his beloved Gurudev pervading everywhere. His complete self experiences him. All the senses concentrate on him alone. Day and night the eyes see the entire universe filled with him only, the ears hear incessantly the sweet mantra *Guru Om*, the tongue relishes uninterruptedly that juicy nectar of Shri Guru's sweet name, and the mind enjoys the presence of the loving Guru everywhere.

Gurudev is sound in the ether. He alone is felt in the touch of the air. He is the light in fire, the sweetness of water, and the fragrance of the earth—he alone fills everything. He is seen in all beings in various forms. Everywhere the blessed devotee feels the same joy and nothing but joy. The entire universe is full of Gurudev Shri Nityananda, who is love—delightful and full of nectar. Everything is filled with joy, beauty, and sweetness. Devotee and God are sweet; the object and the subject are both lovable. You and I and all are blissful. All that is pervaded by delightful and lovable Lord Shri Guru is sweet. The lover of the Guru, having attained this state, remains absorbed in the nectar of divine love for all time; yet that state of love is indescribable. Love is the very essence of the innermost core of *bhakti*. Love is also an immensely valuable and cherished possession, and it is indeed the highest limit of joy and happiness. There is nothing beyond this, and that nothingness itself is Nityananda, eternal joy and bliss, who presently resides in the form of a statue in the Guru Mandir of Gurudev Siddha Peeth in Ganeshpuri. Even his statue radiates powerful vibrations of his all-encompassing love. Innumerable men and women, *yati* and *muni*, pious and sinful, young and old, happy and miserable still come to have *darshan* of his lifelike and powerful image. They consider themselves blessed, are satisfied, and leave feeling happy.

5

Japa Yoga

In this Kali Yuga (the Dark Age), *nama japa,* * or repetition of the name of God, is a highly potent means of acquiring divine knowledge and success in any endeavor. The secret of Japa Yoga is very profound and difficult to explain. It has limitless powers, by means of which aspirants can attain the highest yogic state with ease, however difficult, unknown, or incomprehensible it may be. Japa Yoga occupies an important place in the sphere of spiritual science. It has been practiced from time immemorial by all classes of society the world over, by all traditions, religions, and faiths such as Vedic, Smarta, Tantric, Jain, and Buddhist, each in their individual ways. The practice of *nama japa* affords equal protection to all without distinction. It serves everyone—high or low, *bhakta* or yogi, *jnani* or meditator, rich or poor, foolish or wise, poet or artist, physically disabled or morally fallen. *Namasmarana,* remembrance of God's name, can be fruitfully pursued by spiritual aspirants in any condition. As a seeker progresses in his practice, his love for God increases day by day and he gradually earns the grace of the Lord. His faith deepens, and he develops greater enthusiasm and courage in his spiritual pursuit.

The practice of *japa* is indeed a divine, nectar-like experience of spiritual endeavor, perfect in itself. It is well said:

*Mantra, *japa, shabda,* and *namasmarana* are all synonyms.

shukasanakādi siddha-muni-jogī,
nāmaprasāde brahmasukha-bhogī.

Shukadev, Sanak, and other enlightened sages and
yogis tasted the bliss of Brahman, or Supreme Reality, through the name of God.

The significance of *nama japa* can never be adequately described. Lord Krishna says in the *Bhagavad Gita, yajnānām
japayajno'smi*—"Of all the *yajnas,* I am the *japa yajna*"—
showing the superiority of *japa* among all offerings of prayers
and sacrifices. *Japa* is *maha yajna,* a great sacrificial prayer,
and it is the form of the Lord Himself. *Nama jcpa* is also
known as Japa Yoga (union through *japa*) because by destroying the veil of separation which has disunited us from
our real, divine, and blissful Self, it reunites us with Supreme Reality, or God; it lets us enter the realm of our
blissful Self. In other words, it reunites the soul with that
Brahman which is One without a second. This is also
known as realization of the all-pervading Consciousness.

In Maharashtra there once lived a great saint, Namdev,
who was a Prema yogi, a yogi of love. He advocated the
practice of *namasmarana* with intense love. Namdev epit-
omized his teaching in this way:

nāmā mhane nāma,
chaitanya nija dhāma.

The name of God is the very abode of Consciousness.

Thus, *nama japa* is at once a means and an end. That
it is the best means to God-realization has been very
eloquently emphasized by great men and women through
the ages: Gorakhnath, Gopichand, and Bhartruhari—who
were Hatha yogis; Janaka, Sanaka, Markandeya, and
Bhagiratha—Raja yogis; Narada, Dhruva, Prahlada, and
Shuka—Mantra yogis; Vrishabhadeva, Jadabharata, and
Ajagar—Laya yogis; and Mira, Janabai, Draupadi, and
Chaitanya Mahaprabhu—Prema yogis. These great men

and women of Truth, who were indeed selfless and impartial, highly acclaimed Japa Yoga as a straight, royal road for those seeking salvation. The path of yoga known as Surat Yoga, which was followed by saints and seers in the Middle Ages, is the same as Vak Yoga, that is, Japa Yoga.

The difficult exercises of Ashtanga Yoga, the intricate rituals of *yajna* (to accomplish which one has to master textual passages of Vedic prayers, etc.), the all-absorbing contemplation on the sublime thought "I am Brahman" of Jnana Yoga (in which one must first attain purity and subtlety of the mind before one is fit to pursue the path), and the cultivation of all-exclusive, supreme devotion and love for God, a prime qualification of Bhakti Yoga—all these paths are learned only by strenuous effort and therefore are not easy for everyone to fulfill. But aspirants who practice continuous remembrance of the mantra given them by their Guru can, without great effort, reach the same spiritual consummation as in all these paths:

> *japata pavanasuta pāvana nāma;*
> *apane vasha karī rākheu rāma.*

> Repeating the holy name, Hanuman won Rama's love for himself.

Japa Yoga is the best means of achieving the ultimate fruit aspired to by followers of different spiritual disciplines. Shri Shankaracharya* said:

> *sakalapurushārthasādhanam sukhasampādyam*
> *alpaprayāsam analpaphalam.*

> *Japa* is the most effective way of achieving the fourfold aims of life. It can be practiced with ease, and it yields great results with the least effort.

---

*Shri Shankaracharya wrote a commentary on the *Vishnu Sahasranam* which is worth studying. There is also a work in Marathi called the *Namachintamani*, in two parts. These works deserve to be read by all practitioners of Japa Yoga.

He further stated:

*himsādipurushāntaradravyāntara-
deshakālādiniyamānapekshatvam.*

Practice of Japa Yoga does not require one to do a
sinful act like killing [of animals for sacrifice]. It
does not require help from any person or spending
any money; nor is it limited to a fixed place or
time.

The grace of a Guru alone is enough to enable one to practice Japa Yoga with very little effort. It is well said in the
Mahabharata:

*japastu sarvadharmebhyah paramo dharma uchyate;
ahimsayā cha bhūtānām japayajnah pravartate.*

Japa is the highest of all religious practices because
japa yajna can be fulfilled nonviolently, that is,
without killing of animals for sacrifice.

The great law giver Manu said that by practice of *japa*
alone a person can achieve success in his spiritual endeavor
and attain perfection. He may or may not practice any
other discipline. Indeed, all *siddhis* (that is, the material
gains, such as health, wealth, and happiness, and even perfection that one longs to achieve) are acquired through Japa
Yoga. The scriptures on mantra, *jnana, bhakti,* and yoga, as
well as the science of astrology formulated by sages, are all
valid. They are subtle and profound. Only our own power
of comprehension, which has inherent limitations and var-
ies in degree, leads some of us to doubt the validity of these
scriptures.

The science of astrology tells us that the actions of previ-
ous births confront us in our present birth in the form of
prarabdha (destiny), and we have to reap their fruit, sweet or
bitter, during this lifetime. Astrology describes the influence of the twelve signs of the zodiac on one's life, as well
as the relative positions of planets in these signs, thus indi-

cating one's good or bad fortune. The future is seen according to the strength of the twelve houses in the horoscope. For instance, those whose *dhana sthana* (house of wealth) is not strong or pure lead a life of penury. Those whose *putra sthana* (house of children) is weak either do not have a son born to them, or have a son who goes astray. Similarly, those whose *jaya sthana* (house of partnership) is not good either do not get married, or, if they do, become unhappy with their spouse. All this is true. Thus, as long as each of the twelve houses in the horoscope is not pure, one will not derive the full benefits signified by each. Yet a *sadhaka* who practices *nama japa* with faith, devotion, and love is bound to derive the full benefits of all houses of the horoscope. This is because as he progresses in his *japa,* each of the houses gradually undergoes complete purification. First, his *tanu sthana* (house of physique) is purified and his body becomes healthy. Then comes the purification of *dhana sthana.* A poor seeker comes to enjoy prosperity, and a rich one becomes virtuous. The *parakrama sthana* (house of valor) then becomes pure. The seeker develops qualities of courage, fortitude, and willpower whereby he becomes devout, religious, and fearless. The purification of *vidya sthana* (house of learning) endows the seeker with scholarship and erudition. That is why, when the process of purification of all the *sthanas* in the horoscope is accomplished by means of *japa,* the Japa yogi begins to enjoy inner peace, happiness, and material well-being, and experiences the supreme bliss of communion with God as well. *Nama japa* is a veritable *kalpavruksha* (wish-fulfilling tree) or *kamadhenu* (celestial cow) to those who lead a worldly life. It is no exaggeration to describe *nama japa* as *paramachintamani* (a gem which yields anything desired).

MANTRA
Its Meaning and Potency

According to the *Mantra Shastra,* there are as many as 70 million mantras. Many of these, such as *Om Namo Narayanaya, Ram Ramaya Namah, Klim Krishnaya Namah, Om Namah Shivaya, So'ham, Shivo'ham,* and the *Devi Navarnava* mantra, are said to lead one to the realization of Brahman.

Continuous remembrance of such a mantra is *japa.* Repetition of a mantra received from a Siddha Guru (a perfect Master) eventually leads one not only to the vision of one's chosen deity or knowledge of Supreme God, but also to the much coveted Self-realization, and yields happiness and all kinds of rewards. In fact, the mantra is powerful enough to take one very close to God. It is even capable of transforming a human being into God. Every spiritual aspirant should remember this fact. The highest aim of mantra is Supreme Shiva, or the Self, which is pure Consciousness.

It has been truly said, *ādau bhagavān shabdarāshihi*—"In the beginning, God was in the form of word"—which means that Parashiva, the Supreme Being, is of the form of sound. Sound is as pervasive as space. The *chidakasha,* that is, the space of Consciousness in the heart, is the seat of God. The sound of *japa,* once it enters the *chidakasha,* has the potency to impart the highest enlightenment. In the *Mahanirvana Tantra* it is said:

> *mantrārtham mantrachaitanyam yo na jānāti sādhakah,*
> *shatalaksham prajapto'pi tasya mantro na sidhyati.*

This means that a person who practices *japa* without understanding its meaning and potency will not derive the fruits thereof, even if he repeats the mantra 10 million times. It is therefore necessary to understand the mantra fully:

*pruthang mantrah pruthang mantrī
na siddhayati kadāchana;
jnanamulamidam sarvam
anyathā naiva siddhayati.*

If a mantra is recited with the idea that the mantra
and its reciter are different, it will never yield perfection. This is basic. Without this knowledge
about mantra, one will never achieve the result.

One cannot complete the *sadhana* of Japa Yoga, that is,
one cannot attain the highest fruit of practicing *japa,* if one
lacks proper understanding and believes that the mantra, its
deity, and its reciter are separate entities. In reality:

mantrāh mananatrānarūpāhā shivādabhinnasvarūpāhā.

This means that the mantra has the potency to protect
one who contemplates it; it is not different from Shiva. It
makes one who constantly reflects on it attain oneness with
Lord Shiva. That is why mantra is considered a form of
Shiva.

*vāchyavāchakayorabhedopachārāt
mantro mantradevatā;
evam mantrimantradevatāsu
ārādhyārādhakabhāvena
pruthagdhīh siddhim naiti.*

Worship is done with an understanding of the identity of the named and the word which expresses the
name; the mantra is itself the deity of the mantra.
However, the idea that the reciter of the mantra
and the deity of the mantra are different, and a
feeling of distinction between the worshipper and
the worshipped, will not be fruitful.

No distinction should be made between the deity of the
mantra and the mantra that is recited. *Japa* and the deity
whose *japa* is practiced are one and identical. The means
and the end to be achieved are not different. The mantra

itself is the deity invoked by the mantra. The successful completion of the repetition of the mantra calls for an inner feeling or understanding that the mantra, its reciter, and the deity connoted by the mantra are one and the same. Even a partial feeling of distinction among these three will bring very meager results for a Japa yogi.

One who has sought all the details about mantra and its practice from the Guru who has given the mantra will achieve immediate results in his endeavor to perfect mantra *japa*. A Mantra yogi must know and understand the supremely blissful God in the form of sound:

> *mantrā varnātmakāh sarve,*
> *sarve varnāh shivātmakāh.*

> All mantras are composed of syllables, and all syllables are the very soul of Lord Shiva.

All mantras are composed of letters, and all letters constitute mantras. They are thus Lord Shiva; that is, they are completely of the form of Lord Shiva. In fact, the real nature of mantra is Maheshvara, the Great Lord. The Lord is mantra in another form. Lord Shiva said to Parvati, the mother of the universe, *mantro madrūpaha varānane*—"O beauteous one, mantra is My very form." When a seeker recognizes the mantra as the very form of Lord Shiva, it rises forth spontaneously in the *chidakasha* and helps him to attain identity with Shiva. For this reason, mantra is identical with Maheshvara. Indeed, mantra, the name of God, is as perfect as God Himself.

The great *rishis*, realized souls with deep insight, said that when a person becomes thorough in *shabda brahma*, that is, in the practice of mantra *japa*, the knowledge of the highest Reality dawns on him. Thus, to attain the Supreme, which is beyond words, one has to make use of *shabda* (the word, or mantra) and then go beyond the realm of words. It is also said in the scriptures that this universe came into being through the word and is sustained by the power of the

word. If one wishes to go beyond creation, then the word is
the vehicle. Therefore, in Japa Yoga, one is advised to
reach the Supreme Reality through the means of *shabda*.

In mundane life, too, we learn and understand everything, and carry out all our dealings, through words, that is,
through speech. News and reports about what is happening
in the world are all communicated to us through words.
When a person expresses his feeling or experience through
speech, it is his own Self that is being revealed through the
spoken word. Hence, a word is the very person who speaks
it. Similarly, the all-knowing mantra, which is the Guru's
own Self, resides in his heart in a live form as *prana* and
apana. Therefore, the mantra imparted to a disciple, even if
small, carries with it great potentiality, like the seed of a
banyan tree.* The mantra given by the Guru, although
seeming to be mere syllables, has the divine potency to
awaken the highest yoga in a disciple. It has the power to
burn up completely a *sadhaka's* accumulated *karmas*. On entering a *sadhaka*, the mantra is capable of transforming him,
of making him worthy of attaining oneness with Shiva.

Great sages who were *mantradrushta* (seers of mantra)
spoke of two types of mantras: *jada*, or inert, and *chaitanya*,
or alive. That which is completely free in all respects and
which infuses life into everything is *chaitanya*. That which,
by reason of its full independence, infuses life into the sun,
the moon, the stars, the lightning, and the elements,
which activates the mind, the intellect, and *prana* (vital
force) in their respective functions by animating them, and
which, though itself changeless, through that inaction activates the entire inner and outer world consisting of both
the animate and the inanimate, is none other than the
Lord of the mantras, the Parashiva Paramatman, the highest aim of that extremely pure and live mantra. Just as the

---

*The mantra to be chosen for *japa* should not be very long, because
it is difficult to harmonize the repetition of a long mantra with the
breathing process.

mantra is Parashiva, the Lord of the mantra is Parashiva, and Shri Guru is also Parashiva.

When the Guru has made his mantra divine and alive, it is known as *chaitanya* mantra. This mantra is perfect, liberating, a precious divine gift, as well as the giver of all types of powers. Along with the mantra, the Guru's *atma-shakti*, the power of his soul, enters a *sadhaka* who prac-tices *japa* regularly. A *chaitanya* mantra is obtained from a Siddha Guru, through his grace. By continuous repetition of such a mantra, the *sadhaka's* own *atmashakti* is awakened. By the awakening of the inner Shakti, known as Kundalini, all the *chakras* are pierced. After the piercing of the *chakras*, all the impurities of the body are completely removed. Then the flow of *prana* and *apana* is equalized, and the *sushumna* (the central *nadi*) becomes active. When the *sushumna* fully unfolds, the seeker becomes one with Lord Shiva. As a result of the union of Shiva and Shakti in the *sahasrara*, one who has finally established himself in that ever-blissful Shiva is recognized as a Siddha; such an at-tainment is called the state of Siddhahood. The *Shiva Sutras* say, *siddhaha svatantra bhāvaha*—"Such a one enjoys perfect freedom." Just as seed begets seed, so does an aspirant who obtains a *chaitanya* mantra from a Siddha Guru reach the state of a Siddha at the completion of his spiritual practice. On attaining this state, he enjoys complete freedom; no vestige of dependence ever comes over him again. His mind, senses, mental and psychic tendencies, and intellect are now under his control and can no longer agitate him. The Adi Guru, or first preceptor, Parashiva, initially im-parted His Chiti Shakti, which is full of wisdom and bestows the highest bliss, to His devoted disciple. That disciple in turn imparted it to his disciple, and he to his disciple, and so on. Thus, through the Guru–disciple tra-dition which has come down to us from time immemori-al, the creative power (*kriya shakti*), the immanent aspect of the changeless and inactive Parashiva, continues to be active. This activity belongs to yoga. That is why a mantra should always be obtained from a Guru.

The Self, or *atman*, of the Guru never changes in its perfection. Whoever merges with the Guru becomes one with his Self, and that Self does not become diminished, severed, warped, deteriorated, or even increased. Always remaining in the same changeless, irreversible state, the Guru transforms his disciples just as the philosophers' stone turns iron into gold. Like a magnet, he activates the divine Shakti lying inert in his disciples. And like the holy waters of the Ganges, he makes his disciples as pure as he is and thereby makes his disciples' disciples perfect Gurus like himself. Thus, one who is identical with Lord Shiva in every way, who has imparted to other spiritual aspirants the divine Shakti by which they can bring their disciples to perfection, and who is thoroughly capable of giving the divine authority of *gurupad* (Mastership) to others, is alone Shri Guru. He is the transmitter of *mantravirya* (essence of mantra) to his disciples. There is not the slightest difference between the Guru and Lord Shiva:

> yo guruh sa shivah prokto
> yah shivah sa guruh smrutah;
> ubhayorantaram nāsti
> gurorapi shivasya cha.

This means that a worthy disciple, who by obtaining the divine grace of the Master has become the Guru, is Shiva. Indeed, Shiva becomes the Guru, and then no difference between the two exists. The Guru is none other than the manifested form of Lord Shiva: *sa gururmatsamah prokto mantravīryaprakāshakah.* Here Shiva Himself says that the Guru who radiates the potency of mantra is like Shiva. Truly speaking, he is Shri Guru who always remains the same at all times, in all places, and in all things and who is all-pervading. According to the maxim *shivo bhūtvā shivam yajet,* one who first thinks himself to be Shiva, then wor-

ships Shiva, and ultimately becomes Parashiva, is the Guru.
The entire universe belongs to him because all animate and
inanimate things of the world are created, maintained, and
dissolved by him. Thus, although apparently inactive, he is
active. He, being the Guru, is the benevolent God of his
disciples. Just as the boundless ocean makes all the streams
of water that flow to it like itself, in the same way the Guru
who has transmitted the essence of mantra, which is his
own blissful Self, into the disciple's heart and transformed
him into his own likeness is indeed Shri Guru, the knower
of the potency of the divine mantra. He is the destroyer of
the worldly bondage of his disciples. The Guru takes a
human form to bestow the highest good on devotees. By
entering his disciples in the form of the mantra, the Guru
makes his life identical with the mantra. Just as a caterpillar
is transformed into a butterfly, so does a *sadhaka* who has
received the Siddha mantra attain perfection and become
like Lord Shiva.

> *tadākramya balam mantrāh sarvajnah balashālinah;*
> *pravartante'dhikārāya karanānīva dehinām.*

Thus, it is said in the *Spanda Karika* by Vasuguptacharya
that mantra contains all the powers such as omniscience.
This power of mantra starts the process of yoga in a *sadhaka*
and gives him all the *siddhis;* thus, mantra is the begetter of
Kriya Yoga. Both the Guru and his mantra are the forms of
Shiva. If a *sadhaka* performs mantra *japa* while identifying
himself with the Guru who has imparted the mantra, the
mantra itself, and the great Lord Shiva, then the mantra
instantly activates inner yogic processes and very soon he
becomes like Lord Shiva.

JAPA IN THE FOUR BODIES

Without true knowledge there is no liberation from the
cycle of birth and death. An ancient *rishi* said, *jnānāt tu*

paramā gatihi—"Through knowledge, you attain the final beatitude." And again, the Lord says in the *Bhagavad Gita:*

> *na hi jnānena sadrusham pavitramiha vidyate.*
>
> Truly, there is nothing in this world as purifying as knowledge.

Vedanta, which contains the knowledge of eternal truths, is supreme among scriptures. It describes the four bodies *(sharira)* of the soul *(jivatman)*: the gross *(sthula)*, the subtle *(sukshma)*, the causal *(karana)*, and the supracausal *(mahakarana)*. Vedanta explains that through *jnana*, as the *sadhaka* is freed from the first three bodies one by one and reaches the fourth body—the transcendental state, the abode of the Self—he fully visualizes Lord Shiva, who is pure, nonattached, and *turiyatita* (beyond the fourth state). To understand the exact location, size, form, and nature of the different bodies is not at all easy. The soul's gross body is about five feet in size, is composed of five elementary constituents, and is red in color. The subtle body is about the size of a thumb, is white in color, and is located in the region of the throat. The causal body resides in the heart, is black in color, and is about half the size of the joint of the thumb. The fourth body is blue in color and about the size of a grain of lentil or a tiny spot. It is very difficult to be convinced of all this without a direct experience. Yet for a Japa yogi there is no difficulty; it can be understood easily and naturally. This is because as one progresses in the practice of *japa*, one is gradually induced into a radiant state of *tandra*, a superconscious state in which one is neither awake nor asleep. In *tandra*, these bodies are clearly perceived.

When *japa* of the gross body, as recited by the tongue, goes deeper inside and begins to be repeated in the throat, it is known as *japa* of the subtle body. When this happens, the *sadhaka* should understand that Japa Yoga has purified the gross body and has now entered the subtle body. Here the number of mantra repetitions increases many times.

During *japa* in the throat, the *sadhaka* experiences a divine *tandra.* In this state he experiences a kind of blissful sleep and sometimes has visions of gods, goddesses, the Guru, and other Siddhas and saints. This second body, also called *sukshma sthana,* is where dreams take place. By *japa* in the subtle body one's faith in Japa Yoga deepens, and now and again one feels happy within the heart. The reward that one gets from repeating the mantra a hundred times in the gross body, in a wakeful state, can be obtained by one repetition of the mantra in the subtle body. The *sadhaka* at this stage enjoys excellent health and lightness of body. Certain inner activities occur in the regions of the heart and navel. The *japa* of the throat goes on continuously day and night, like a fine stream of oil. It can be practiced by the *sadhaka* even while he attends to his daily, routine work. When *japa* is going on in the subtle body, the *sadhaka* quite naturally does all his work with skill and ability, for he receives guidance or inspiration from within. He even has a glimpse of the third (causal) body, which is black. In the final stage, *japa* in the subtle body enables the *sadhaka* to glimpse a number of things in his inner being, and these glimpses or revelations are significant.

When the subtle body is thoroughly purified, *japa* goes still deeper. Now it occurs in the heart, which is the location of the causal body. This region is also known as *sushupti sthana,* or the seat of deep sleep. Some even call it *shunya sthana,* or the void. That the causal body resides in the heart is the experience of all. The knot of ignorance *(hrudayagranthi)* is also in this region. The seeds of all the evils which cause one to go round and round in the cycle of birth and death are also there. When *japa* is being repeated in the third body, the *sadhaka* becomes aware of the subtle vibrations of the syllables of the mantra. Now he is even more cheerful and enthusiastic than before and performs *japa* with increased love.

The number of mantra repetitions here is also more than those in the region of the throat. Here one repetition is equal to one hundred in the throat region. The *japa* of the heart region is very powerful. It not only strengthens the body and adds luster to the eyes and the face, but also makes the *sadhaka* do adventurous things. During *japa* in the heart, the heat increases in the head and the *sadhaka* feels warmth in all his limbs. Usually, he falls asleep during *japa,* yet the repetition of mantra maintains its continuity. Even when the *sadhaka* is busy with worldly work, *japa* continues internally. At this stage, he feels detached from everything and therefore attains proficiency in any work he undertakes.

When the required number of mantra repetitions of the third body is completed, *japa* moves to the navel region. From the spiritual point of view the navel region is of great importance. When *japa* moves to this region, the blue, lustrous fourth body is perceived within. During this stage, the *sadhaka* experiences various visions of divine lights. The light of the fourth body is indicative of the vision of God. This is also the light of Brahman, sometimes described as the supreme light of *japa.* Seeing this light, the *sadhaka* becomes very contented, hopeful, and enthusiastic and devotes more time to his spiritual endeavor. At this stage, the different states of *jnana, bhakti,* and yoga arise. As soon as all the impurities such as desire and attachment are burned up in the fire of *japa* of the navel region, the *sadhaka* has visions of Siddhas, Gurus, gods and other heavenly beings, sacred rivers like the Ganges, the sun, moon, and other luminous bodies, and holy places like Shri Shailam, all in the state of *tandra.* Naturally, with all these experiences he feels very hopeful of attaining the spiritual goal of ultimate fulfillment.

During *sadhana* in the fourth body, the vibrations of *japa* are also felt in the head. By the power of *japa* in the navel

region, all the hidden *shaktis* are awakened. Then, as a result of *japa*, the divine sound *(nada)* is heard in the head,
and the *sadhaka* listens to it with great wonder. At this
stage, as a gift from the Guru, the *sadhaka* receives a sort of
mantra in the form of continuous awareness of his own Self
(*svasvarupa-anusandhana*). This mantra is a kind of medal
from the benign and gracious Guru. Since the *sadhaka* has
carried out his spiritual practices with unflinching faith and
reached the fourth abode of *japa* through the strength of
gurukrupa, and because he has fulfilled the purpose for
which he was initiated, the Guru is highly pleased. Therefore, in token of his delight and as a tribute to the disciple's
worthiness, he gives a mantra which enables the disciple to
realize his real Self. Immediately thereafter, the disciple is
entirely transformed. Now *japa* is practiced through the
unmanifest speech. The *sadhaka* does not have to make any
effort to do this *japa;* it goes on automatically by the Guru's
grace. This kind of *japa* is described as *ajapa-japa*, which the
sadhaka joyfully listens to with a quiet, calm mind. Kabir
expressed his own experience of this effortless *japa:*

> *hamārā japa kar rām,*
> *hama baithe ārām.*

Rama practices my *japa* while I sit relaxed.

For this *japa*, one has neither to move the tongue nor to
make any attempt at focusing the mind, and there is
neither hardship nor even weariness.

The *ajapa-japa*, or the *japa* of the fourth body, is actually
neither *japa* nor action nor any kind of spiritual practice.
At this stage the *sadhaka* feels, "I am perfect," and this
feeling comes naturally to him. This *japa* is *nirgunanirakara*,
which means that it has no particular form or quality.
There is no differentiation such as God and devotee, yoga
and yogi, or mantra and reciter. Instead, there is a blissful
feeling of indivisible unity with the universe. Just as a king

feels, "This is my kingdom," wherever he goes in his own territory; just as the sky hears its own echoes everywhere, in all directions; just as an actor, though playing various roles feels only himself in them; similarly, a *sadhaka* who has the awareness "I am perfect" sees his own Self pervading every-thing. This is the highest goal of *gurukrupa*, the culminat-ing fruit of *sadhana*.

Such a blessed *sadhaka* loses his individuality. Initially, he perceived the world as full of misery and hardship and as a place of transient enjoyments. But when transformed by the practice of Japa Yoga, he has the experience that, being one with the Guru, he is ageless and immortal. To him the universe now appears to be a paradise, and the world, the Sadguru, and all fellow beings look benign like Shiva. In the vast garden of this universe, he proclaims, "I am Shiva," for, indeed, he has become Shiva. He neither loves nor hates, because for him all likes and dislikes have be-come Shiva, and the universe has become the form of Shiva. With the worshipful knowledge of the universe as Lord Shiva, he cheerfully fulfills his remaining *prarabdha*. Constantly practicing the *japa* of unity, he enters the holiest region of the fourth body; transcending even the fourth state, that is, becoming *turiyatita*, he realizes that only he and nothing else exists. Just as one who is on the ocean sees nothing except water on all sides, similarly, a Japa yogi, devoid of the feeling of mine and yours, interior and exterior, higher and lower, sees only his own Self everywhere.

"I am Shiva. There is nothing different from Shiva, nothing other than Shiva"—thus convinced that I, you, he, and all are Shiva, and merging in Shiva, Shiva be-comes Shiva. This is Japa Yoga's highest reward; this is the pinnacle of Guru's grace; this is the final result of the *sadha-ka's* spiritual fortitude; this is religion put into practice; this is visiting the holiest Shiva temple of Kailas on one's pil-grimage to ultimate liberation.

That the *sadhaka* has all these different experiences, that he has a vision of the Guru and even converses with him in the blue *mahakarana,* or fourth body, is not an exaggeration. The unmanifest speech, which spontaneously arises in the fourth body, is *chitimaya,* that is, pure Consciousness. Chiti Shakti is entirely independent. The *Pratyabhijna-hridayam* says, *chitihi svatantrā vishvasiddhihetuhu* — "Supremely independent Chiti is the cause of the manifestation of the universe."

Chiti, the nonseparable soul power of the Supreme Shiva, is independently powerful. She is the cause of the creation, sustenance, and dissolution of the world, from the highest being to the inert, insentient earth. Chiti governs all the activities of the entire universe. There is nothing beyond or higher than Chiti, the Absolute Consciousness; nor is She different from Supreme Shiva. The universe comes into existence because of Her unfolding, and when She turns inward in the process of involution, the universe dissolves. Chiti is the cause of the entire objective world, and Chiti is also the fulfillment of all endeavors. Chiti is the substratum of the universe. The world, both the visible and the invisible, is created by Chiti without any material or instrumental cause. Chiti Herself takes the form of the universe, but Her innate nature as pure Consciousness does not change. Without the help of any object or any other power, Chiti alone and independently carries out Her work; She assumes infinite forms and creates the universe. Just as the various organs of the physical body are formed from one drop of semen, just as the fruit, flower, and leaf of the entire banyan tree lie hidden in its one small seed, in the same way this Chiti displays a sort of grand dance in the universe. By becoming both cause and effect and by donning universal and individual form, She enjoys Her greatness perpetually.

With such power, it is not difficult for the Chiti Shakti to appear in a *sadhaka's* visions, assuming various forms and guiding him as well. Therefore, what a *sadhaka* sees outside in the world he also sees within himself, because the individual body is the form of the universe. The direct experience of a *sadhaka* is the only proof of the validity of this truth.

It is invariably true that the Guru, in a subtle form, resides in the two-petaled lotus located between a *sadhaka's* eyebrows. The Guru is in fact the same as the grace-bestowing Chiti which pervades the universe. When the required number of mantra repetitions is completed at this center, the Guru gives the *sadhaka* a mantra within the fourth body. No matter where the disciple may be staying, it is very easy for the Chiti Shakti to appear to him in a vision in the form of his own Guru. This is neither an overestimation of Her power, nor a figment of imagination, nor even magic.

My revered Gurudev, Bhagavan Shri Nityananda, used to guide his devotees in far-off countries such as England and America. Once he even gave guidance in a vision to a man traveling by plane. The Chiti Shakti is unfathomable in Her potency and full of infinite miracles. At any time, under any circumstances (favorable or otherwise), Chiti assumes marvellous forms of many in one or of one in many. Depending on a *sadhaka's* sincerity, faith, and confidence, supereminent Chiti makes him fearless and, according to his feelings and understanding, even instructs and guides him assuming the form of the Guru.

When a yogi reaches the highest realm of yoga, his awakened Kundalini, having united with Shiva in the *sahasrara*, penetrates and becomes diffused in every nerve, every cell, and every hair of his body. Thus, when the Kundalini has completely pervaded the four bodies, the five concentric sheaths (of physical matter, vital energy, mind, intelligence, and bliss), and the three states (waking, dreaming, and deep sleep), She firmly stabilizes the yogi's insight in realizing oneness everywhere. The *Shiva Sutras* say, *yathā atra tathā anyatra*, which means that what is here is everywhere. To the yogi, therefore, any place is the same. For him heaven, earth, and the netherworld, Paris, London, New York, and Tokyo, China, Russia, and Tibet are all one—Shiva's empire.

Once a disciple of such a yogi was doing the *sadhana* of meditation in America and running a business at the same time. This *sadhaka* was in urgent need of some spiritual guidance. One day when he sat for meditation, his Guru appeared and instructed him in English. The disciple was extremely pleased that his Guru was so great. He wrote a letter to us stating that his Guru, the great yogi, visited him in America and, after having had a good talk with him, returned to India. I replied that this was no cause for surprise. Such phenomena occur through the Chiti Shakti, which equally and fully pervades everywhere.

Chiti, the supreme power, knows all languages. All knowledge, all science, all wisdom are the creations of Her vibrations. The science of yoga, together with all its branches, is merely a small particle of Chiti's infinite being. Chiti is in all respects the Guru, the Master, of every religious and spiritual path. Molding Herself in an approachable form, She instructs and guides a *sadhaka* in the language that he understands. It is not at all difficult for Her to do so. Although the world, consisting of movable and immovable things, is the same in the form of the divine Shakti, She makes the *sadhaka* see the same in an infinite variety.

From the same condensed milk a variety of sweets, of different shapes, colors, and flavors, are prepared. A variety of figures are painted by an artist on the same canvas, with the same brush and the same color. Onlookers may distinguish them as pictures of a man, a child, a cow, a horse, a flower, and a fruit, but in truth the artist is one, the canvas is one, the color is one, and the brush is one. The artist has no feeling of good or bad toward any figure. He believes that he has painted many in one. To paint a new figure or to erase a painted one raises no question of either like or dislike, delight, sorrow, or anxiety. Similarly, the divine Chiti creates the world of infinite forms by Her own power, without any particular motive or expectation.

This mysterious Chiti, taking the form of a mantra, resides in the syllables of the mantra. Therefore, such mantras are Chiti Herself. As a *sadhaka* practices more and more mantra *japa*, Chiti burns up his feeling of limited individuality in the fire of mantra and elevates him to the experience of oneness with the infinite Self. Since mantra is Chiti, it also has Chiti's capacity for creation, sustenance, and dissolution. The truth of all this can be known only through Self-realization.

However much one may say or write on the subject of mantra *japa*, it will always remain incomplete, for there is no end to it. *Japa* gives shelter to all; there are no barriers to its practice; and through it the desired ends, powers, and perfection can be achieved. Through *japa*, liberation is attained in this very life. *Japa* is divine and the practitioner of *japa* attains divinity. *Japa* leads to the highest fulfillment.

6

The Path
of
Knowledge

Self-realization is not attained without knowledge, for knowledge is the very nature of God. The Supreme Being blazes forth as knowledge. Without knowledge it is not possible to have the final experience. God, in fact, is ever present within our inner being. He pervades the entire universe, sentient as well as insentient. He always shines in the heart. It is God who makes our minds active. Although He has always been with us, we are still ignorant of Him. Therefore, our need for knowledge is great.

If the nature of the inner Self is knowledge, why do we not immediately perceive the Self? Our inner Self is undecaying, perfect, eternal, and self-effulgent—then why are we in such a plight? Why have we not discovered our own nature? What has rendered the ever-enlightened ignorant, Consciousness matter, the perfect imperfect, and the blissful miserable?

The cause of all this is ignorance. Because of our own ignorance, we have shrunk from sublimity to pettiness, from infinity to finitude, from wholeness to fragmentation. When our ignorance is completely eradicated, we become fully enlightened. Just as night can be ended by day alone, cold by heat, and sins by virtuous deeds, so ignorance can be destroyed only by knowledge. *Japa*, austerities, fasting, sacrifices, and other rituals cannot dispel ignorance com-

pletely. It is knowledge that fully reveals the nature of God.
The light of the soul is indeed the light of knowledge.

Where are you looking for God—God who is eternally
present in all places, all moments of time, and all things? In
what corners are you searching for the One who is ever-
existent? It is all right to strive to obtain something that
you do not have or that exists in a remote region. But how
can you seek that which you always have and which is the
closest, the innermost? In which holy place, cave, or forest
retreat can you find Him? Manpuri said:

> kyom bana-bana dhūmdhata sāīm,
> sāīm ghata māhīm,
> koī pūraba koī pashchima,
> guru bina upajata nāhīm.

> Why are you looking for God from forest to forest
> when He exists within the heart? One looks for
> Him in the east, another in the west, but He can-
> not be seen without the Guru.

I, too, searched intensely for Him in caves, mountains,
and forests. But when I came to Bhagavan Nityananda, I
perceived Him at once. I do not remember in exactly how
many temples I had sought Him or in how many shrines I
had meditated on Him to no avail. I prayed in so many
different temples, but only hours slipped by and I was still
without peace. I practiced severe austerities, but they only
emaciated my body without taking me closer to God. I
practiced pranayama and struggled with other Hatha Yoga
techniques for a prolonged period, but I only became proud
that I was a good yogi; I did not obtain peace. I constantly
repeated the divine name. I sang devotional songs—even
with professional singers—until I was weary. I told beads,
put the sacred mark on my forehead, and let my hair grow
into matted locks. But all that I had were the beads, the
sacred mark, and the long locks. Time passed without any
real gain.

Then I set out in search of a guide. One naked one turned out to be addicted to the pipe, while another asked me to pierce my ears in the Shaivite manner. One told me to smear my body with sacred ash, another to wear a black garment. Yet another suggested saffron robes. One instructed me to observe silence. Thus, my search continued until I was exhausted. Then I wandered all by myself, pondering the mysteries of life. In the course of those wanderings, I ran into an unusual, naked saint named Zipruanna. He was very great. Although he appeared to be a fool to worldly-minded fools, he was omniscient. He seemed a naked mendicant only to those who were spiritually naked, being without knowledge. However, he was the owner of a vast treasure of wisdom—a true millionaire. I loved him at first sight. We became friends. What a combination! One was a naked *fakir* while the other was a well-dressed, modern renunciant. He said, "O you crazy one, God is within! Why do you seek Him outside?"

I said, "Instruct me."

"That is not for me to do," he replied. "Go to Ganeshpuri. Your treasure lies there. Go and claim it."

I went to Ganeshpuri and met Nityananda Baba, the supreme *avadhuta*. I was overjoyed. No—I was fulfilled. After a bath in the hot springs, I went for his *darshan*. He was poised in a simple, easy posture on a plain cot, smiling gently. His eyes were in the *shambavi mudra* (eyes open but gaze directed within). What divine luster glowed in those eyes! His body was dark, and he was wearing a simple loincloth. He said, "So you've come."

"Yes, Sir," I answered. I stood for a while and then sat down. There I realized the highest. I am still sitting there. Where shall I go now?

Peace cannot be had in the absence of the Guru, nor can self-contentment or inspiration. When I obtained Sadguru Nityananda, I obtained all.

Nityananda said, "Why look for the indwelling Lord outside? Look within your own being. Your Rama, your peace, lies inside. Meditate."

Through meditation I received the Guru's grace, and then I found Him easily. He whom I had been seeking in holy centers, caves, forests, mantras, and robes was disclosed by my Guru to be my own Self, seated in my own heart.

Thus, God cannot be realized without the Guru even though He is manifest. Therefore, obtain true vision from the Guru and you will see Him. The Lord showed Himself to Arjuna as being present in his own heart. If someone were to ask me what Krishna gave to Arjuna, I would say that the Lord, in His role as the Supreme Guru, granted Arjuna the eye of knowledge. Krishna dwelled within Arjuna, but because Arjuna lacked the eye of wisdom, he could not see Him who was his own all-pervading Self. As a result he had neither peace nor courage. When he received the inner eye from the Guru, he at once discovered God in his own heart.

Friends, do not seek God; seek the Guru. God abides within you. The Guru is the one you need to grant you the divine vision of the inner light. And that divine vision is the highest knowledge. Yoga, devotion, *japa*, and austerities cannot equal it. But it must be directly revealed by the Guru. Mere words are of no avail. It is the direct, immediate experience which alone matters. Without knowledge you cannot get anywhere. Lose the ego and find the Self. Merge your separate existence into the Universal Being. Then you will find peace stretching infinitely on all sides.

You will see very little if you merely close your eyes and begin to search. You will only complain that it is all dark. But the truth is that it is all light. It is only your eyes which are blind. In fact, all those who try to see without the eye of knowledge are blind. Behold the inner witness, the spectator who watches all the activities of your waking state while remaining apart from them; who dwells in the midst of all action, good or bad, knowing it fully and yet remaining uncontaminated by it; who is that supremely pure, perfect, and ever-unattached Being. Try to know Him who does not sleep during the state of sleep, remaining fully aware and witnessing all the events of the dream world. On waking up one may say, "I slept very well. I had a dream about a beautiful temple." Are these words uttered by the one who slept? He says that he saw a temple while he slept! What an enigma! O friends, behold the spectator who remains awake while you sleep, poised far from sleep. Who is He? He is the pure witness, the attributeless One. He is the Supreme Being. He is within you, but you look for Him outside.

Human beings have four bodies, one within the other. They should be explored. What exists in the fourth body? That is the realm of pure Consciousness, of the beloved Self delighting in itself—the land of perfect contentment, of total freedom from anxiety, of the highest realization. Plunge within through meditation, surveying the inner territory with the eye of knowledge. Nanakdeva said:

bāhara bhītara eka hī jāno,
yaha guru jñāna batāī.

The same One pervades within and without. This has been revealed by the knowledge received from the Guru.

It is true that what is inside is also outside. Explore it for yourself. Consider an analogy: The earth is present everywhere. Wherever you go, you remain on its surface. Similarly, the world is in God and God is in the world. Where are you looking for Him? Why do you exhaust yourself unnecessarily? Your penance is futile. You only become weary in your search for Him. You are picking up cow dung for nothing.

An aspirant once approached a Guru and said, "Venerable Master, I take refuge in you. Please instruct me."

This saint was a simple person with an all-pervading outlook. He said, "Thou art That—God dwells within you."

"I know this already," the student said. "Please teach me
something more."

The teacher replied, "Brother, I have only one teaching.
If you want a different teaching you will have to find a
different teacher."

The seeker went away in search of another Master. This
time he approached a big one who had attained full knowledge, having mastered the science of the Absolute and
gained a direct experience of it. The Master was sitting in
silence. The seeker said, "Sir, kindly impart knowledge to
me. I am without any knowledge of the Self."

The Master asked, "Where have you come from?"

The seeker told him the name of his earlier teacher. As
soon as the Master heard the name, he realized that without service, knowledge imparted to this seeker would never
bear fruit. So he said, "You will have to serve the Guru for
twelve years. Then you will receive true knowledge."

The seeker accepted this condition and said, "Knowledge
is all I want. Please tell me in what manner I may serve
you."

The Master called the manager of the ashram and asked,
"Is there a vacant job in the ashram?"

The manager said, "All the work is going well. There is
only one job available, and that is picking up cow dung."

The Master told the seeker, "You may have the job of
picking up cow dung. At the end of twelve years, at the
consummation of service, you will obtain knowledge."

The seeker picked up dung and cleaned the cowshed
every day. After twelve years had gone by, he went to the
Master and said, "Gurudev, I have completed my service.
Grant me knowledge now."

The Guru said, "Thou art That. All that there is, is the
Self, and it is you."

When he heard this, the seeker was satisfied. He had no

doubt about the truth of the Guru's words. Yet he asked, "I knew this before; I even heard it explained. Why, then, did you make me pick up cow dung?"

The Guru replied, "Your experience should answer your question. Since you performed *guruseva* for twelve years with faith and devotion, you now understand these words. It is the reward for your service."

The world is as one sees it. It reflects one's own state. If the world is regarded as real in itself, it becomes filled with sorrow, misery, want, and anxiety. The world appears to be mundane because of one's own ignorance of the play of the Spirit. The world deceives us when we consider it to be simply the world as we see it. However, once we experience the blissful sport of Consciousness, the world is transformed into a haven of bliss.

Because of our ignorance of the nature of a rope, we actually perceive it as a serpent. If we see the rope as a rope, our perception is true and our peace is not disturbed. We remain happy and without fear. But if we see wrongly, we see the serpent and fall victim to fear and agitation.

A person becomes his own enemy and begins to torture himself. He himself becomes a sinner and then groans. He himself serves the poison of ignorance to himself and thus commits suicide. While he is hostile to himself, he blames others. Why do you commit suicide for lack of knowledge? Give up your illusions and see yourself as you really are. Uplift yourself by means of knowledge. Serve the nectar of wisdom to yourself. Achieve greatness. The soul dwells as the perceiving Consciousness in every being. Reflect on the inner Truth. Explore your own depths. Direct your seeking within. Revel in your own being.

The poet Ramchandra told a story which illustrates that one becomes what one thinks. Its meaning is profound. Whatever one wishes for under the *kalpavruksha* (the wish-fulfilling tree) one gets. Once a slothful, foolish, and destitute fellow approached this tree. Finding it shady and beautiful, he sat under it. The surroundings were fascinating. The man began to wish, "If only there were a bungalow here!" Immediately a bungalow appeared. "If only there were a garden around it!" A garden also appeared. Then followed cushions, pillows, and beds. A kitchen, equipped with gold and silver utensils, also materialized and then a table covered with sweet delicacies. "If only there were a woman here!" the man thought. And at once a beautiful maiden came along.

Then this dull-witted fool began to think, "Whatever I wish for comes into being. Can there possibly be a devil around?" As soon as he entertained this thought, a frightful devil appeared. The fellow was scared out of his wits. He began to think, "Most likely this devil will eat me up!" Immediately the devil pounced on him and devoured him.

O dear ones! This world is not a vale of sorrow. It is neither a transient phenomenon nor a void. It is neither a field of action nor illusory, neither real nor unreal nor an abode of differences. It is the beautiful playground of Lord Shiva; it is not inert matter but the divine abode of gods. To the ignorant and blind it is transitory, but to the enlightened, to those filled with devotion to the Guru, it is the sport of the Absolute. For the unbelieving, the world is a vale of tears, but for the believing and detached who are filled with love for God, it is the manifestation of His love. For the wise, for perfect and ecstatic beings, this world is a divine, intoxicated play. Know the world fully; know it as it is. Do not confuse a post with a thief and run around in sheer panic. Do not become trapped in the performance of naming and sacred-thread ceremonies. Do not consider this divine play to be the son of a barren woman. Do not get ready for a bath with soap and towel, regarding as real the waters of a mirage. The world, in fact, is Shiva; it is Kailas; it is Rama. This indeed is Vaikuntha. This world is an expansion of the highest Shiva, a conscious playground of the love of Universal Consciousness. It is nothing but Chiti.

You, He, and I are all permeated with Chiti. Whatever is, is Chiti. Look with this all-embracing vision, the vision of knowledge. What nectars flow here! Look at the beauty of the beloved Universal Mother.

Understanding is determined by knowledge. Attitude is shaped by understanding. Peace and joy arise in the mind according to one's attitude. Take the case of an ordinary soldier. If he becomes a lieutenant, he feels more important. As he rises through the ranks from a lieutenant to a major and then to a brigadier general and finally assumes the position of commander-in-chief, his power increases progressively and so does his awareness of his stature. If he becomes the president of his country, his authority is far more pervasive and he also feels far more important. Actually this person remains the same throughout. What changes then? It is his own idea of himself. He felt insignificant while he was a soldier, but now he considers himself not a soldier but the president of his country. Similarly, if you give up the wrong view of yourself as a trivial, destitute, inferior, begging, and imprisoned creature and instead begin to feel that you are Shiva, the all-pervasive soul, that you are perfection itself, how much greater your joy will be! Stop looking upon yourself as a limited individual. Become firmly anchored in the sense of your own pervasiveness, of your ability, greatness, and purity.

Bhagavan Nityananda used to say, "All are Rama—great as well as small. Rama is yours. Rama is mine." This is truly the essence of Vedanta. He had seen the mystery of things. He was fully aware of the inner observer, the one who understands. His skill in practical affairs was based on the Vedantic vision of unity in diversity. Sometimes he would say, "Neither go toward another, nor move away from him. Neither become hostile to anyone, nor run to strike up friendships. Do not rush to accept a gift, nor become entangled in the pride of giving. Do not look for faults in others, nor congratulate yourself on singing their praises.

Shun evil completely, but do not at the same time become attached to good. Every moment utter, 'O Rama! O Rama!' Never forget Rama. Think of God and not of yourself. Regarding praise and blame as brothers, continue to repeat, 'O Rama! O Rama!' Destitution should be as welcome as riches. Both of them are the fruits of past actions. They affect one who identifies himself with them. Remain detached from both since they are the consequences of destiny determined by *karma* and are the will of God. Do not prefer one to the other, and thus avoid being pseudo-wise. Do not set yourself up as a worthless middleman who snatches from the rich and distributes to the poor. Do not become agitated by either the riches of the wealthy or the poverty of the poor. Constantly utter, 'O Rama! O Rama! O Rama!'

"Putting on the guise of the love of Rama, you claim to be a follower of Rama, yet you resort to the malicious distinction of high and low. Open your eye of knowledge and see what you should do. You have sought initiation in the outlook of equality, but your actions reek of partisanship, of inequality. This is a mockery of devotion and knowledge. Do not behave like this. It is Rama who appears in different guises. Continually repeat, 'O Rama! O Rama!'

"This world is Rama's playhouse. There cannot be a king without subjects. There cannot be riches without poverty. There cannot be day without night. The universe is based on duality. Duality will vanish only when the universe vanishes. O renunciant, why have you given up repeating the name of Rama and turned to other things instead? Why should you take sides in any way? Realize that it is Rama who weeps and Rama who laughs. Why do you abandon the name of Rama? Keep repeating the divine name of Rama. Rama's will alone works. Much of your life has already been spent fruitlessly. Not much time is left before you die. Why do you perceive differences in Rama? All is Rama; all is Rama indeed."

This is what Nityananda Baba used to say. His teaching embodied the essence of Vedanta, embracing unity in diversity and diversity in unity. Let your understanding be enlightened by Vedanta or you will be subject to remorse.

Once an extremely kind person went to a sage and began to talk to him about a plan he had devised to abolish poverty. The sage told him, "Brother, this world is dominated by the law of *karma*. When did God entrust you with the task of changing it?" He added, "Just as wealth is an illusion, so is poverty. Friend, repeat every moment, 'O Rama! O Rama!'"

Do not forget that Self-knowledge, or God-realization, is your aim. Some people turn away from practical life under the illusion that it is an obstacle on the path to God. But later they unwittingly get caught in the same trap. It is very difficult to escape the net of past impressions. A holy pretender is not even aware of how his holiness betrays him, how it makes him conceited, thus plunging him into ignorance. Ordinarily it is exceedingly difficult to save oneself without the grace of the Supreme Sadguru. Generally a so-called wise devotee gradually loses his wisdom when he has to apply it to worldly affairs. To one with the eye of devotion, all are Gopal. Kings, millionaires, the poor, the foolish, soldiers, poets, actors, and artists—all these are only different players in the divine drama. One's outer form or circumstances are determined by one's *karma*. However, for a devotee, the enjoyment of objects in the external world does not bring him closer to Rama. He finds Rama only when he is absorbed in the inner Self. Indifferent to riches as well as poverty, both of which are barren and joyless, he keeps his attention focused on his Self reposing in his heart. A true worshipper of Rama's name is so absorbed in divine love and knowledge that he does not attach any importance to the wealth of the entire universe or to that of the worlds of Brahma, heaven, Indra, or the moon. Equanimity, perfection, friendship with his own Self, courtesy arising from the awareness of the Self in all, and nobility of character constitute his true wealth. To see distinction in knowledge and devotion is nothing but party politics. Love and knowledge will survive only if they are kept apart from politics; otherwise, they will die.

The Vedantic philosophy of equality is based on true vision. Pleasure and pain, gain and loss, wealth and poverty are all consequences of *karma*. They pertain only to the gross body, whereas insight is the transcendental wealth of the supracausal body. How can those without knowledge and devotion, those who are slaves of money, outer honors, degrees, and titles, obtain this wealth? O renunciant, turn away from the external world and plunge within. There lies your true kingdom. You are the emperor of transcendental realms. Try to rise above the illusion of differences. Acquire the vision of oneness, of sages, seers, and other enlightened beings—the vision of pure knowledge, the vision of the divine play. Be guided by the pure Vedantic insight, by the experience of transcendental bliss, and by the knowledge of the true nature of God. It is only this vision of unity which enables one to realize the Godhead, which puts an end to human suffering, and which raises human beings to the divine plane. If you become the sovereign of your own inner kingdom and are led by divine inspiration, you will see Rama everywhere. You will see Shyam stretching from east to west, and Shiva from north to south. This is the kingdom of *avadhutas*, the boundless expanse of pure joy. Obtain this treasure at this very moment. It is the strong and beautiful abode of bliss. Let your mind be focused on it. This is the goal of the knowledge of the enlightened, of the devotion of devotees, of the meditation of meditators—the true imperishable state which is worth attaining. This is truly the gift of the grace of Sadguru Nityananda.

Glossary

Asana: (1) Any one of various bodily postures practiced to strengthen the body, purify the nerves, and develop one-pointedness of mind. The yoga texts describe eighty-four major *asanas.* (2) A seat or mat on which one sits for meditation.

Ashram: A spiritual community.

Ashtanga Yoga (or Raja Yoga): The eightfold yoga expounded by Patanjali in his *Yoga Sutras.* The eight steps are: (1) *yamas:* the practice of five moral virtues—nonviolence, truthfulness, celibacy, nonstealing, and noncovetousness; (2) *niyamas:* the practice of five regular habits—purity, contentment, austerity, study, and surrender; (3) *asana:* posture; (4) *pranayama:* the regulation and restraint of breath; (5) *pratyahara:* withdrawal of the mind from sense objects; (6) *dharana:* concentration, fixing the mind on an object of contemplation; (7) *dhyana:* meditation, the continuous flow of thoughts toward one object; (8) *samadhi:* complete absorption or identification with the object of meditation, meditative union with the Absolute.

Atman: See Self.

Avadhuta: A saint who lives in a state that is beyond body-consciousness and whose behavior is not bound by ordinary social conventions.

Bhakti: Divine love; devotion to God.

90

Brahmin: The first caste of Hindu society, the members of which were by tradition priests, scholars, and teachers.

Chaitanya: The fundamental Consciousness, which has absolute freedom of knowing *(jnana shakti)* and doing *(kriya shakti).*

Chakra (lit. wheel): Any one of seven major energy centers, or subtle nerve plexuses, in the human body.

Darshan: (1) Spiritual philosophy. (2) Seeing God, an image of God, or a holy being.

Dharana: See Ashtanga Yoga.

Dhyana: Meditation.

Ekanath Maharaj (1528–1609): Householder poet-saint of Maharashtra. The illustrious disciple of Janardan Swami, he was renowned in his later life for his scriptural commentaries and spiritual poetry.

Guru: A spiritual Master who has attained oneness with God and who initiates his disciples and devotees into the spiritual path and guides them to liberation.

Hatha Yoga: A yogic discipline by which the *samadhi* state is attained through union of the *prana* and *apana* (ingoing and outgoing breath). Various bodily and mental exercises are practiced in order to purify the *nadis* and bring about the even flow of *prana.* When the flow of *prana* is even, the mind becomes still. One then experiences equality-consciousness and enters into the state of *samadhi.*

Jnaneshvar Maharaj (1275–1296): Foremost among the saints of Maharashtra and a child yogi of extraordinary powers. He was born into a family of saints, and his older brother Nivrittinath was his Guru. His verse commentary on the *Bhagavad Gita—Jnaneshvari—*written in the Marathi language, is acknowledged as a great spiritual work. He took live *samadhi* at the age of 21 in Alandi, where his *samadhi* shrine continues to attact thousands of seekers.

Jnani: (1) A follower of the path of knowledge. (2) An enlightened being.

Karma: Action; accumulation of past actions.

Kriya: Gross (physical) or subtle (mental, emotional) purificatory movement initiated by the awakened Kundalini.

Kriya Yoga: See Siddha Yoga.

Kundalini (*lit.* coiled one): The primordial Shakti, or cosmic energy, that lies coiled in the *muladhara chakra* of every individual. When awakened, Kundalini begins to move upward within the *sushumna,* the subtle central channel, piercing the *chakras* and initiating various yogic processes which bring about total purification and rejuvenation of the entire being. When Kundalini enters the *sahasrara,* the spiritual center in the crown of the head, the individual self merges in the Universal Self and attains the state of Self-realization.

Laya Yoga: The practice of merging the mind in the Absolute through absorption in sound and lights.

Mahavakyas (*lit.* great statements): Four statements containing the essence of the wisdom of the Upanishads. They are "Thou art That," "This Self is Brahman," "Consciousness is Brahman," and "I am Brahman."

Mudra: (1) *Mud,* "joy"; *ra,* "to give"; called *mudra* because it gives the bliss of the Self. (2) Seal, because it seals up *(mudranat)* the universe into the being of transcendental Consciousness. (3) Hatha Yoga posture and manipulation of different organs of the body as an aid in concentration. (4) Symbolic signs made with the fingers in ritualistic worship and classical dance.

Nadi: Channel in the subtle body through which the vital force flows.

Nadishuddhi: The purification of the *nadis,* which happens spontaneously in Siddha Yoga as a result of *shaktipat.*

Nanak (Guru Nanak or Nanakdev; 1469–1538): The founder and first Guru of the Sikh religion.

Nirguna: Without attribute; the formless aspect of God.

Nirvikalpa: The highest state of *samadhi,* beyond all thought, attribute, and description.

Prana: The vital force, specifically, the vital air in the breathing process.

Pranayama: See Ashtanga Yoga.

Prarabdha karma: Accumulated past actions, the fruits of which have become one's destiny. *Prarabdha* must be experienced; it cannot be erased.

Pratyabhijnahridayam (*lit.* the heart of the doctrine of recognition): A concise treatise of twenty *sutras* by Kshemaraja which summarizes the Pratyabhijna philosophy of Kashmir Shaivism. It explains the process by which Universal Consciousness becomes an individual soul through a process of contraction and the means by which our true nature as Consciousness can be realized.

Pratyahara: See Ashtanga Yoga.

Puranas (*lit.* ancient legends): Eighteen sacred books containing stories, legends, and hymns about the creation of the universe, the incarnations of God, and the instructions of various deities, as well as the spiritual legacies of ancient sages and kings.

Rishi: An inspired sage.

Sadhaka: An aspirant on the spiritual path.

Sadhana: The practice of spiritual discipline.

Saguna: With attribute; the aspect of God with form.

Sahasrara: Thousand-petaled spiritual center at the crown of the head where one experiences the highest states of consciousness.

Samadhi: A state of meditative union with the Absolute. See Ashtanga Yoga.

Self: The divine Consciousness within each human being which is one with the Universal Consciousness.

Shankaracharya (788–820): One of the greatest of India's philosophers and sages, who expounded the philosophy of absolute nondualism (Advaita Vedanta). In addition to his writing and teaching, he established *maths* (ashrams) in the four corners of India.

Shiva: (1) A name for the all-pervasive Supreme Reality. (2) One of the Hindu trinity, representing God as the destroyer; the personal God of the Shaivites. In His personal form, He is portrayed as a yogi wearing a tiger skin and holding a trident, with snakes coiled around His neck and arms.

Shiva Sutras: A Sanskrit text that Shiva revealed to the sage Vasuguptacharya. It consists of seventy-seven aphorisms, which were found inscribed on a rock in Kashmir. It is the major scriptural authority for the philosophical school of Kashmir Shaivism.

Shyama (*lit.* the dark one): A name of Krishna, so called because of his dark blue complexion.

Siddha: A perfected yogi; one who has attained the highest state and become one with the Absolute.

Siddha Yoga: The yoga that takes place spontaneously within a seeker whose Kundalini has been awakened by a Siddha Guru and that leads to the state of spiritual perfection.

Spandakarikas: A collection of verses on the dynamic apsect of Consciousness; commentary on the *Shiva Sutras* attributed to Vasuguptacharya.

Sushumna: The central and most important of the 72,000,000 *nadis*; located in the center of the spinal column extending from the base of the spine to the top of the head. The six *chakras* are situated in the *sushumna,* and it is through the *sushumna* channel that the Kundalini rises.

Sutra (*lit.* thread): A short aphoristic phrase which conveys lengthy philosophical material in a highly condensed form.

Swami: Title of a *sannyasin*—a monk in the Indian tradition.

Tantra: An esoteric spiritual discipline in which Shakti, the creative power of the Absolute, is worshipped as the Divine Mother through the practice of rituals, mantras, and *yantras* (visual symbols). The goal of tantra is attaining Self-realization through Kundalini awakening and through uniting the two principles, Shiva and Shakti.

Tukaram (1608–1650): Great poet-saint of India; author of thousands of devotional songs.

Turiyatita: The state beyond *turiya;* the supremely blissful state. of complete freedom from all duality and the awareness of the one Self in all, the final attainment of Siddha Yoga.

Upanishads: The teachings of the ancient sages that form the knowledge or end portion of the Vedas. The central doctrine is that the Self of a human being is the same as Brahman, the Absolute. The goal of life is realization of Brahman.

Vedanta: A philosophical school founded by Badarayana, which contains the philosophical teachings of the Upanishads and investigates the nature and relationship of the Absolute, the world, and the Self.

Vedas: Very ancient and authoritative revealed scriptures of India.

Yajna: A sacrificial fire ritual in which different materials such as wood and *ghee* (clarified butter) are offered to a fire while Vedic mantras are recited; any work done in the spirit of surrender to the Lord.

Yamas and *niyamas:* Restraints *(yamas)* and observances *(niyamas)* that are considered vital to one who is pursuing a yogic life. See Ashtanga Yoga.

Gurudev Siddha Peeth, Swami Muktananda's Ashram, Ganeshpuri, India.

OTHER PUBLICATIONS

By Swami Muktananda

The Perfect Relationship   The Guru/disciple relationship
Secret of the Siddhas   Swami Muktananda on Siddha Yoga and Kashmir Shaivism
Does Death Really Exist?   A perspective on death and life
Mystery of the Mind   How to deal with the mind
Reflections of the Self   Poems of spiritual life
Play of Consciousness   Muktananda's spiritual autobiography
Satsang with Baba   (Five Volumes) Questions and answers
Muktananda-Selected Essays   Edited by Paul Zweig
Meditate   Muktananda's basic teaching on meditation
In the Company of a Siddha   Muktananda talks with pioneers in science, consciousness and spirituality
Siddha Meditation*   Commentaries on the Shiva Sutras and other ancient texts
Mukteshwari I & II   Poetic aphorisms
I Am That   The science of Hamsa mantra
Kundalini: The Secret of Life   Muktananda's teachings on our innate spiritual energy
Small books of aphorisms: I Welcome You All With Love, God Is With You, A Book for the Mind, I Love You*, and **To Know the Knower.**

About Swami Muktananda

A Search for the Self   by Swami Prajnananda. Swami Muktananda's biography
Muktananda Siddha Guru*   by Shankar (Swami Shankarananda). Introduction to Muktananda and his teachings.

Other Books

Introduction to Kashmir Shaivism   The philosophy most closely reflecting Muktananda's teaching
Understanding Siddha Yoga, Volumes I & II   Textbooks on Siddha Yoga
Nectar of Chanting   Sacred chants sung regularly in Muktananda's Ashrams. Sanskrit translation with transliteration
Lalleshwari   Poems of a great woman saint
Hatha Yoga for Meditators   A detailed guide to Hatha Yoga as taught in Swami Muktananda's Ashrams
Shree Guru Gita   Word-by-word translation with transliteration and original Sanskrit

Publications

Gurudev Siddha Peeth Newsletter   Monthly from Muktananda's Ashram in India
Shree Gurudev Vani   Annual Journal by devotees
Siddha Path   Monthly magazine of SYDA Foundation

* Also available in Braille   Complete with photographs

If you want more information about these books, write to SYDA Bookstore, P.O. Box 605, South Fallsburg, N.Y. 12779.

MAJOR CENTERS AND ASHRAMS

There are over 300 Siddha Yoga Meditation Centers and residential Ashrams around the world. They all hold regular programs which are free and open to the public. Many of them also conduct Siddha Yoga Meditation Intensives and Introductory Programs. Contact any of the following major Centers for the location of the Center nearest you.

UNITED STATES

SYDA Foundation New York
P.O. Box 600
South Fallsburg, New York 12799
Phone: (914)434-2000
　　　　(212)247-5997

SYDA Foundation Ann Arbor
1520 Hill
Ann Arbor, Michigan 48104
Phone: (313)994-5625
　　　　994-3072

Siddha Yoga Dham Atlanta
P.O. Box 183
Atlanta, Georgia 30301
Phone: (404)377-7834

SYDA Foundation Boston
Fernwood Road—Manor House
Chestnut Hill, Massachusetts 02167
Phone: (617)734-0137

**Siddha Yoga Meditation
Ashram Chicago**
2100 W. Bradley Place
Chicago, Illinois 60618
Phone: (312)327-0536

Siddha Yoga Dham Cincinnati
157 Ridgeview Drive
Cincinnati, Ohio 45215
Phone: (513) 821-3629

**Siddha Yoga Meditation Center
Costa Mesa**
431 East 20th Street
Costa Mesa, CA 92627
Phone: (714)631-4446

Siddha Yoga Dham Gainesville
1000 SW 9th Street
Gainesville, Florida 32601
Phone: (904)375-7629

Siddha Yoga Dham Hawaii
P.O. Box 10191
Honolulu, Hawaii 96816
3807 Diamond Head Circle
Honolulu, Hawaii 96815
Phone: (808)732-1558

**Muktananda Meditation Center
Siddha Yoga Dham Houston**
3815 Garrott
Houston, Texas 77006
Phone: (713)529-0006

SYDA Foundation Manhattan
324 West 86th Street
New York, New York 10024
Phone: (212)873-8030

Siddha Yoga Dham Miami
256 S.W. 12th Street
Miami, Florida 33130
Phone: (305)858-5369

SYDA Foundation Oakland
P.O. Box 11071
Oakland, California 94611
1107 Stanford Avenue
Oakland, California 94608
Phone: (415)655-8677

**Siddha Yoga Dham
Oklahoma City**
1215 N. Miller
Oklahoma City, Oklahoma 73107
Phone: (405)949-1931

Siddha Yoga Dham Philadelphia
6429 Wayne Avenue
Philadelphia, Pennsylvania 19119
Phone: (215)849-0888

Siddha Yoga Dham Seattle
1409 N.E. 66th
Seattle, Washington 98115
Phone: (206)523-2583

**Siddha Yoga Dham
Washington, D.C.**
5015 16th St. N.W.
Washington, D.C. 20011
Phone: (202)882-4377

AUSTRALIA

Siddha Yoga Dham Melbourne
202 Gore Street
Fitzroy, Melbourne VIC 3065
Australia
Phone: (03)419-6299

Siddha Yoga Dham Sydney
1 Warrenball Ave.
Newton NSW 2042, Australia
Phone: (02)519-7540

CANADA

Muktananda Meditation Society
Vancouver
P.O. Box 2990
Vancouver, B.C. V6B 3X4
Canada
Phone: (604)734-7181

Muktananda Meditation Center
Mississauga
6789 Segovia Road, Mississauga
Ontario L5N 1P1, Canada
Phone: (416)826-4512

ENGLAND

Siddha Yoga Dham London
1 Bonneville Gardens
London SW4 9LB England
Phone: (01)675-4105

FRANCE

Siddha Yoga Dham France
7 Rue du Plaisir
93400 St. Ouen
Paris, France
Phone: (1)258-51-35

GERMANY

Siddha Yoga Dham Germany
Fifchergasse 5
6050 Ossenbach – Main
Phone: 0611-86 1260

INDIA

Gurudev Siddha Peeth
(WORLD HEADQUARTERS)
P.O. Ganeshpuri (Pin 401 206)
Dist. Thana
Maharashtra, India

Shree Gurudev Ashram
New Delhi
Bhatti Village, Mehrauli Block
c/o Khanna, Claridges Hotel
New Delhi South, India 110030

ISRAEL

Siddha Yoga Dham Jerusalem
Harazim St. 10/24 Beit-Hakerem
Jerusalem, Israel
Phone: (02)520184

ITALY

Siddha Yoga Dham Rome
Via Germanico 107
00192 Rome, Italy
Phone: (06)385-063

MEXICO

Siddha Yoga Dham Mexico City
Apartado Postal 41-890
Mexico 10 DF Mexico
Phone: (905)286-1676

NETHERLANDS

Muktananda Siddha
Meditation Center
Amsterdam
Da Costakade 116 I hoog
1053 XB Amsterdam, Netherlands
Phone: (020)85-1596

NEW ZEALAND

Siddha Yoga Dham Canterbury
351 Gardiners Road
Christchurch 5, New Zealand

PUERTO RICO

Siddha Yoga Dham Puerto Rico
48 M. Rivera Street
Cabo Rojo 00623 Puerto Rico
Phone: (809) 832-7164

SPAIN

Siddha Yoga Dham Barcelona
Gran Via, 434 #3
Barcelona 15, Spain
Phone: (93)325-3197

Siddha Yoga Dham Madrid
Apdo 42 081
Madrid, Spain
Phone: (91)448-8349

SWEDEN

Siddha Yoga Dham Stockholm
Kapellgrand 17
S-116 21 Stockholm, Sweden
Phone: (08)435-709

SWITZERLAND

Muktananda Siddha
Meditation Center Bern
Brunngasse 54, 3011
Bern, Switzerland
Phone: (031)22.59.63

VENEZUELA

Quinta Mukta Venezuela
Urbanización Macarena Sur, 93
Los Teques, Venezuela
Phone: (032) 43-755